30 MINUTE CURRIES

30 MINUTE CURRIES

Atul Kochhar

I dedicate this book to my best friend – my son, Arjun.
He has an amazing, loving personality, and this little person's
selflessness has taught me so much in this life. He always puts
his loved ones before himself. And he loves his football and
rugby, being a British lad, but adores his cricket (except we
are rivals when England is playing India).

His participation in cooking the recipes for this book
has been a huge encouragement to me. He was always coming
up with little ideas of how I should cook a vegetable that he
doesn't usually appreciate so much, and some
of his ideas were brilliant.

He loves his food with the exception of vegetables like broccoli
and Brussels sprouts – however we are working together to turn
that around! I am convinced that I will find him behind the stoves
in the cooking lines very soon – he has the right attitude
and passion to be a cook.

He has taken after both of his grandfathers so much, and has
strong likes and dislikes, but he can be persuaded with positive
conviction so there is never a dead end with him – there
is always a way!

I love you my son!

CONTENTS

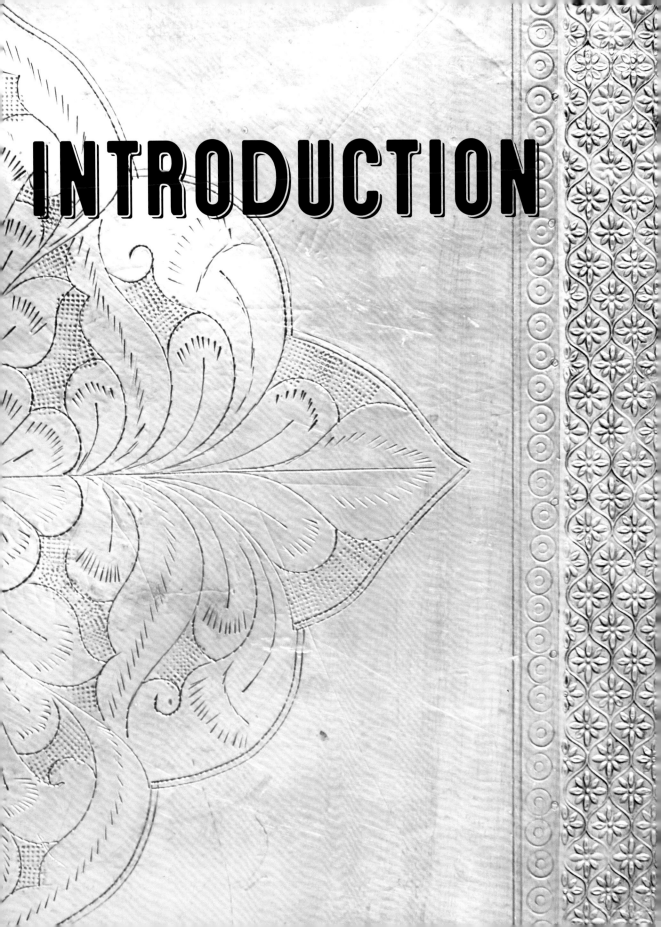

INTRODUCTION

INTRODUCTION

*' Curry in 30 minutes?
You must be joking!
It takes forever. '*

*' Indian food takes forever to cook,
there is too much to prep …
there are too many ingredients …
there are too many steps. '*

*' You are a trained cook
– that's why you can do
it – not a normal person! '*

AND SO IT GOES ON! This is what people have been telling me for ages. Some of these sentiments I sympathise with and some I think are said out of a lack of knowledge. If I can do it, so can you.

So, I am on a mission to entice you all to cook a curry in under 30 minutes. In this book, I have thrown all the 'chef processes' out of the window and I have taken a practical and easy approach to Indian food. In writing the book the most beautiful thing happened and I have ended up with a rich variety of recipes that I have always wanted to write; the kind of recipes a parent would cook for their children at home. They are healthy, fun and creative, and will encourage you to experiment more. I cooked some of the recipes with my kids, and they absolutely loved it.

I wish every child were a foodie like my princess – Amisha! Little Arjun is bit of a challenge for his mum and gran when they cook vegetarian meals at home. To beat his understanding of soggy, soupy vegetable preparations, I kept the vegetables in these recipes crunchy, zingy and sometimes leafy to tickle his palate with textures and win him over with gentle spice flavours. It worked incredibly well on him – he is a self-professed fan of my carrot-parsnip preparation, among many other creations.

I haven't used any deep-frying at all in this entire book. That's some challenge for a cook, isn't it? I have used simple cooking utensils, all of which are found in a domestic kitchen, I have cooked on a normal domestic stove (induction and gas), and used a normal household oven. I have really tried my best to keep all the recipes straightforward and simple.

Throughout the book I have used vegetables, meat, fish and other common everyday ingredients that are all available in most supermarkets, so you shouldn't find any ingredient overly challenging to source. As for spices, I have used very few and only the most common ones – they're probably all sitting in your cupboards already, or have been for the last few centuries (it's time to change them if they are really old).

I have purposely kept the number of red meat dishes to a minimum partly because some of the cuts are challenging to cook within 30 minutes anyway also because I wanted to take a healthy approach to this book. As such I have used: sunflower oil or rapeseed oil, low-fat yogurt, almost no cream or cheese (other than paneer) and I have included turmeric in many recipes as it is universally seen as a superfood.

I have taken the pain out of cooking by pre-preparing a few things like onion paste, garlic paste and ginger-garlic paste (see the basics chapter at the end of the book), and in many recipes I have used tomato paste in place of fresh tomatoes. This not only helps halve the cooking time, but it also makes cooking these recipes even more fun. I recommend making the pastes in a large enough batch to fit into zip up freezer bags, and freezing them flat in the freezer to maximise space. Alternatively, I suggest you buy an ice cube tray (and use it specifically for the pastes or your ice cubes might taste funny) and freeze the pastes in tablespoon or teaspoon portions. Once frozen, tip the cubes into a freezer bag and store, and when you need a paste, as directed in the recipes, you can just take the amount you need and use it straight from frozen.

I sincerely hope that you will love this book and be encouraged to make your own versions of the recipes I have created. I urge you to use social media and share your method and passion with us all. We learn new things everyday and sharing is caring too!

Atul Kochhar
2017

VEGETABLES AND PULSES

MANGO PICKLE-FLAVOURED AUBERGINE

Baigan Achari

Achari is a common term in Indian cookery to indicate that something has been pickled. Here, I use the traditional mix of pickling spices called panch phoron (page 227) and mango pickle for a tang that really tickles the palate. I absolutely adore this dish.

   Normally I wouldn't add water to aubergine as it cooks, but I do in this recipe to speed up the cooking time. I could have deep-fried the aubergine first to soften it, but I want to keep this family-style side dish as healthy as possible.

SERVES 4 AS A SHARING DISH

2 large aubergines, about 550g
   total weight
3 tablespoons vegetable oil
1¼ teaspoons panch phoron
2 teaspoons ground coriander
1 teaspoon ground turmeric
½ teaspoon red chilli powder, or
   to taste
about 200ml water
5cm piece of fresh ginger
2 tomatoes
1 thick green chilli
1 tablespoon Indian mango pickle
   from a jar – you want to use small
   pieces and some of the oil
fresh coriander leaves
sea salt

Assemble all the ingredients and equipment before you begin. You need a large sauté or frying pan with a lid.

Remove the stem end from the aubergines and halve lengthways, then quarter each half lengthways and cut into bite-sized pieces.

Heat the vegetable oil over a medium-high heat in the pan. Add the panch phoron and stir until the seeds crackle. Add the aubergine and stir until all the oil is absorbed. Add the ground coriander, turmeric, chilli powder and ½ teaspoon of salt, and continue stirring for 30 seconds to cook the spices. Watch closely so they do not burn.

Stir in 100ml of the water, then cover the pan and leave the aubergine to steam-cook, stirring occasionally, for 12–15 minutes until it is softened. Watch closely so the aubergine doesn't catch on the bottom of the pan, and gradually stir in the remaining 100ml of water, if necessary. You want to avoid adding so much water that the aubergine becomes mushy, however.

Meanwhile, peel and finely chop the ginger. Coarsely chop the tomatoes. Remove the stalk from the green chilli, if necessary, then finely chop the chilli. If the pieces of mango in the pickle are large, finely chop them. Chop enough coriander leaves to make about 2 tablespoons.

When the aubergine has softened and is golden, stir in the tomatoes, the green chilli, the mango pickle and oil and 1 tablespoon of the chopped ginger. Re-cover the pan and leave to finish cooking over a medium heat for a further 5 minutes, or until the tomatoes are broken down and the flavours are blended.

Adjust the seasoning with salt, if necessary. Stir in the remaining ginger and sprinkle with the chopped coriander just before serving.

CURRIED MIXED VEGETABLES

Kolhapuri Bhaji

Not for the fainthearted! This very simple curry made with frozen mixed vegetables is typical of food from Kolhapur, in the south-western state of Maharashtra, in that it is very hot and spicy. I serve this with parathas.

Normally spices are toasted over a high heat to activate their natural oils and make them aromatic. Here and in other recipes that contain desiccated coconut I've specified to use a low heat. Always stir constantly and watch closely so coconut does not burn.

SERVES 4 AS A SHARING DISH

2 tablespoons vegetable oil
2 tablespoons Onion Paste
    (page 218)
1 teaspoon Garlic Paste (page 220)
250g frozen mixed vegetables
2 heaped tablespoons Greek-
    style yogurt
350ml water
sea salt

For the Kolhapuri spice powder

2 large dried red chillies
6 cloves
1 cinnamon stick
a small blade of mace
4 tablespoons desiccated coconut
1 tablespoon coriander seeds
¼ teaspoon black cumin seeds,
    or use ordinary
¼ teaspoon black peppercorns

Assemble all the ingredients and equipment before you begin. You need a non-stick pan for toasting the spices, a spice grinder and a large sauté or frying pan.

First make the spice powder. Put the dried chillies into the dry non-stick pan over a low heat. Add the cloves, cinnamon, mace, coconut, coriander and black cumin seeds and peppercorns, and stir until they are aromatic and the coconut is lightly toasted. Watch closely so the chillies and coconut do not burn before the spices are toasted. Tip the mixture into the spice grinder and grind until a fine powder forms. Set aside.

Heat the vegetable oil over a medium-high heat in the sauté pan. Add the onion paste and garlic paste and stir them into the oil for 30 seconds. Add the spice powder and stir for a further 30 seconds. Watch closely so the spices do not burn.

Add the frozen vegetables, season with salt and continue stirring until the vegetables start to thaw. Stir in the yogurt, then add the water, stirring to incorporate all the ingredients. Leave to simmer, stirring occasionally, for 8–10 minutes until the gravy thickens slightly. The gravy will be quite thin at first, but it thickens as it simmers because the coconut in the spice powder absorbs the liquid. Adjust the seasoning with salt, if necessary.

Atul's time-saving tip

As with many of the recipes in this book, the key to having a delicious curry on the table in 30 minutes or less is having a supply of onion paste in the fridge or freezer. It gives you all the wonderful onion flavour without having to spend the time peeling, chopping and then cooking the onion. I always have this in the fridge. The recipe on page 218 tells you how to prepare and store in a large quantity so quick-cooking curries can be second nature.

GREEN AND RED CHILLI CURRY

Mirchi Ka Salan

I love this recipe and have cooked it many times. It's one of the recipes in this book that transports me back to my early days of cooking. It comes from the Hyderabad region, where green chillies are a favourite ingredient. *Salan* is the word from the region for curry. Basically, anything with a sauce will be called *salan*.

I've used the Dutch chillies you find in supermarkets in this recipe, more for their flavours and colours than for heat. You might be tempted to use hotter chillies, but I seriously don't recommend it; they are just so wrong for this dish. If you happen to be a person who doesn't like chillies, you can also make this dish with its tangy gravy, substituting courgettes or just about any vegetable for the chillies.

SERVES 4 AS A SHARING DISH

1 tablespoon vegetable oil, plus extra
  for frying the chillies
¼ teaspoon fenugreek seeds
¼ teaspoon onion seeds
3 tablespoons Onion Paste
  (page 218)
½ teaspoon red chilli powder, or
  to taste
½ teaspoon ground turmeric
150ml Tamarind Liquid (page 223)
15g piece of jaggery or palm sugar
250ml water
6 long thick green chillies
6 long thick red chillies
6 fresh or dried curry leaves
sea salt

For the spice and nut powder

50g blanched almonds
3 tablespoons sesame seeds
2 tablespoons desiccated coconut
1 tablespoon coriander seeds
1½ teaspoons white poppy seeds
1 teaspoon cumin seeds

Assemble all the ingredients before you begin. You need a non-stick pan for toasting the nuts, seeds and coconut and frying the chillies, a spice grinder, a large sauté or frying pan with a lid, a splatter guard and tongs or a slotted spoon.

First make the spice and nut powder. Heat the dry non-stick pan over a low heat. Add the almonds, sesame seeds, coconut and coriander, poppy and cumin seeds, and stir until the coconut turns light golden brown and the spices are aromatic. Watch closely so the almonds and coconut do not burn. Transfer all the ingredients to the spice grinder and blitz until a fine powder forms. Set aside. Wipe out the pan and set aside.

Heat the oil over a medium-high heat in the sauté pan. Add the fenugreek seeds and fry, stirring, until they turn darker. Add the onion seeds and stir until they pop. Add the onion paste and stir it into the oil for 30 seconds. Add the chilli powder and turmeric, season with salt and stir for a further 30 seconds to cook the spices. Watch closely so they do not burn.

Stir in the tamarind liquid, scraping the bottom of the pan. Coarsely chop the jaggery, then add it to the pan with the water, stirring to dissolve the jaggery. Stir in the spice and nut powder, then leave the gravy to simmer and thicken while you prepare and fry the chillies.

Slice each of the chillies in half lengthways, but leave the stalks attached so they remain whole.

Heat enough vegetable oil over a medium heat to thinly cover the bottom of the non-stick pan you used for toasting the ingredients for the spice and nut powder. Add the green and red chillies with a pinch of salt, cover the pan with the splatter guard and fry, turning the chillies over with the tongs once for even cooking, for 5 minutes, or until they are just tender, but not falling apart.

Use the tongs to transfer the chillies to the gravy as they are fried, shaking off any excess oil. Stir in the curry leaves, making sure the gravy goes into the chillies' cavities. Cover the pan and leave to gently boil for 5 minutes, or until the chillies are softened. Adjust the seasoning with salt, if necessary.

To serve, transfer the chillies to a dish and spoon the gravy over.

MUSTARD-FLAVOURED AUBERGINE

Sorse Begun

I love the colour of this unusual Bengali dish. I've given my own twist to the dish by not deep-frying the aubergine chunks, which I think most chefs would do. I think it keeps them lighter, and cuts down on the overall fat. In true Bengali tradition, however, I've included some ghee for richness, but you can use all vegetable oil.

SERVES 4 AS A SHARING DISH

1 large aubergine, or baby
   aubergines, about 275g
   total weight
1½ teaspoons ground turmeric
1½ tablespoons ghee
1 tablespoon vegetable oil
250g Greek-style yogurt
2 teaspoons Dijon mustard
¼ teaspoon red chilli powder, or
   to taste
1 long thin green chilli
1 tablespoon mustard oil
1 teaspoon panch phoron
sea salt
coriander sprigs, to garnish

Assemble all the ingredients and equipment before you begin. You need a large non-reactive bowl, a medium bowl, 2 large sauté or frying pans, one of which has a lid, and a whisk or fork.

Remove the stalk end from the aubergine. Halve it lengthways, then quarter each half lengthways and cut into bite-sized chunks. Transfer the chunks to the non-reactive bowl, and add 1 teaspoon of the turmeric. Season with salt and stir together so the aubergine is coated.

Melt the ghee with the vegetable oil over a medium-high heat in the pan with the lid. Add the aubergine chunks with a pinch of salt and stir for 30 seconds to cook the turmeric. Turn the heat down, cover the pan and leave the aubergine to soften, stirring occasionally, for about 10 minutes until it is tender. The salt will draw out the moisture in the aubergine so it shouldn't stick to the bottom of the pan, but you still have to check and stir occasionally.

Meanwhile, put the yogurt in the medium bowl, add the Dijon mustard, remaining ½ teaspoon of the turmeric and the chilli powder. Season with salt and whisk together. Set aside.

Remove the stalk end from the green chilli, if necessary, then finely chop the chilli. Rinse some coriander sprigs for the garnish.

When the aubergine is tender, heat the mustard oil over a medium-high heat in the other pan. Add the panch phoron and the green chilli and stir until the seeds sizzle. Tip the aubergines into that pan and stir together.

Turn the heat to very low. Add all the yogurt at once and stir until the aubergine is coated. Leave to simmer, uncovered, for 2 minutes for the flavours to blend. Adjust the seasoning with salt, if necessary, then garnish with coriander sprigs and serve.

AUBERGINE AND LENTIL CURRY

Vonkai Pulusu

This was a new recipe for me when I was developing the recipes for the book, and I was very pleased with the flavour and texture. It might look a bit like a mush, but I think you will enjoy it all the same. Frying the lentils is a typical preparation from southern India.

SERVES 4 AS A SHARING DISH

3 garlic cloves
1 large aubergine, about 275g
1 onion
3 tablespoons vegetable oil
1 teaspoon split yellow mung dal
    (moong daal)
¼ teaspoon ground asafoetida
1 teaspoon black mustard seeds
4½ teaspoons ground coriander
½ teaspoon ground turmeric
4 tablespoons water
fresh coriander sprigs
sea salt

For the spice paste

2 cloves
2.5cm piece of cinnamon
1 teaspoon white poppy seeds
1 teaspoon sesame seeds
3 tablespoons frozen grated coconut
3 tablespoons Greek-style yogurt
3 tablespoons Tamarind Liquid (page 223)
1 tablespoon water
15g piece of jaggery or palm sugar

Assemble all the ingredients and equipment before you begin. You need a spice grinder, a bowl and a large sauté or frying pan with a lid.

Peel and slice the garlic cloves. Remove the stalk end from the aubergine and halve lengthways, then quarter each half lengthways and cut into bite-sized pieces. Peel, halve and thinly slice the onion.

Heat the vegetable oil over a medium-high heat in the sauté pan. Add the split yellow lentils and asafoetida and stir until the lentils turn white and the asafoetida sizzles. Add the mustard seeds and stir until they pop. Add the garlic and stir around to flavour the oil. Watch closely so nothing burns.

Add the onion and stir until it is softened, but not coloured. Stir in the aubergine pieces, season with salt, cover the pan and leave to steam-cook while you make the spice paste. The salt draws out moisture from the onion and aubergine to keep everything moist, but check occasionally that nothing is sticking to the bottom of the pan.

To make the spice paste, put the cloves, cinnamon and poppy and sesame seeds in the spice grinder, and grind until a fine powder forms. Tip the spice powder into a bowl, add the frozen coconut, yogurt, tamarind liquid, water and palm sugar, and stir together until the sugar dissolves. Set aside.

Stir the aubergine to make sure nothing is sticking to the bottom of the pan. Add the ground coriander and turmeric and stir for 30 seconds to cook the spices. Stir in the water, which will be almost instantly absorbed, but adds enough extra moisture that nothing should catch on the bottom of the pan.

Increase the heat to medium, re-cover the pan and continue steam-cooking for about 5 minutes until the aubergine is tender.

Meanwhile, rinse and chop enough coriander leaves to make about 2 tablespoons.

Stir the spice paste into the aubergine. Re-cover the pan and leave the aubergine to simmer over a medium heat for 2–3 minutes for the flavours to blend. Adjust the seasoning with salt, if necessary, and stir in the chopped coriander just before serving.

Atul's time-saving tip
Cutting the aubergine into thin pieces and adding salt when it goes into the pan definitely helps it cook faster.

BROCCOLI AND CASHEW CURRY

Hari Gobi Aur Kaju Kari

This recipe comes from Mangalore, a lush, green part of India with large coconut, cashew nut and tamarind plantations, all of which are included in this dish. This is particularly good served alongside chicken and prawns.

SERVES 4 AS A SHARING DISH

1 head of broccoli, about 400g
50g unsalted raw cashew nuts
1 tablespoon coconut oil
1 teaspoon black mustard seeds
12 fresh or dried curry leaves
a pinch of red chilli powder, or to taste
½ teaspoon ground coriander
¼ teaspoon ground turmeric
sea salt

For the coconut paste

1 heaped tablespoon coconut oil
2 large dried red chillies
2 teaspoons coriander seeds
¼ teaspoon fenugreek seeds
4 tablespoons frozen grated coconut
3 tablespoons Tamarind Liquid (page 223)
200ml water

Bring 2 saucepans of water (one large and one small) to the boil and assemble all the ingredients and other equipment before you begin. You also need a food processor fitted with a chopping blade and a large sauté or frying pan.

Cut the broccoli into bite-sized florets. Add the florets to the large pan of boiling water with ½ teaspoon of salt. Return the water to the boil and boil for 2 minutes, or until the florets are tender-crisp. Drain well, shake dry and set aside.

Add the cashew nuts to the smaller pan of boiling water, return the water to the boil and boil for 2 minutes to soften slightly. Drain well and set aside.

Meanwhile, make the coconut spice paste. Melt 1 heaped tablespoon of coconut oil over a medium-high heat in the sauté pan. Add the dried chillies, coriander seeds and fenugreek seeds, and stir for 30 seconds until the coriander seeds crackle and the fenugreek seeds turn darker. Add the frozen coconut, then turn the heat to low and stir for 3 minutes, or until the coconut is beginning to dry. You don't want the coconut to colour, so watch closely. Stir in the tamarind liquid.

Transfer the paste mixture to the food processor, add 3 tablespoons of the water and process until the spices are finely ground. Transfer the paste to the small pan the cashews were boiled in, stir in the remaining water and bring to the boil. Stir in the cashew nuts and leave to simmer over a medium heat until required.

Wipe out the sauté pan. Melt the 1 tablespoon of coconut oil over a medium-high heat in the pan. Add the mustard seeds and stir until they pop. Add the blanched broccoli, the curry leaves, chilli powder, ground coriander, turmeric and ¼ teaspoon of salt, and stir for 30 seconds to cook the spices. Watch closely so they do not burn.

Stir in the coconut paste with the cashew nuts. Keep the heat high and continue stirring until the paste reduces and clings to the broccoli florets and the florets are tender. Adjust the seasoning with salt, if necessary and serve.

CAULIFLOWER AND POTATOES

Gobi Aloo

Cauliflower is one of the very common vegetables in Indian households, especially in the Punjab, where my family comes from. Some people like to add yogurt or water to *gobi aloo*, but for some reason in north India we make it very dry, as in this recipe.

When you boil potatoes, I always suggest you boil extra so you always have some in the fridge. If you intend to cook Indian food regularly, you'll have half the vegetables ready. You can then quickly combine them with so many other ingredients, such as peas, peppers and cauliflower. Cooking the potatoes is half the battle.

SERVES 4

8 well-scrubbed small new potatoes (see Atul's tip, page 29)
2.5cm piece of fresh ginger
2 long thin hot green chillies
1 lemon
fresh coriander leaves
2 tablespoons vegetable oil
1 teaspoon cumin seeds
½ head of cauliflower, about 400g
1 tablespoon ground coriander
1 teaspoon red chilli powder, or to taste
1 teaspoon ground turmeric
250ml water
2 heaped tablespoons Onion Masala (page 222)
¼ teaspoon garam masala
sea salt

Bring a large covered saucepan of salted water to the boil and assemble all the ingredients and other equipment before you begin. You also need a heavy-based saucepan with a lid, a large sauté or frying pan with a lid and a large colander or sieve.

Get the potatoes cooking as quickly as possible, adding the whole potatoes to the boiling water. Be careful that the water doesn't splash you as you add the potatoes. Re-cover the pan and return the water to the boil, then boil, uncovered, for 20–22 minutes until the potatoes are very tender.

Meanwhile, peel and finely chop the ginger. Remove the stalks from the green chillies, if necessary, then finely chop the chillies. Squeeze the juice from the lemon and chop enough coriander leaves to make about 2 tablespoons.

Heat the vegetable oil over a medium-high heat in the sauté pan. Add the cumin seeds and stir until they crackle. Add half the chopped green chillies and half the ginger and stir for about 30 seconds to flavour the oil. Watch closely so nothing burns.

Now, do as my mother did when she was in a hurry – cut the cauliflower florets into bite-sized pieces, dropping them into the pan as you cut. They will start cooking immediately. Add the ground coriander, chilli powder and turmeric. Season with salt and stir for 30 seconds to cook the spices. Watch closely so they do not burn.

Stir in the water, turn up the heat to high, cover the pan and leave the cauliflower to steam-cook while the potatoes finish cooking. Uncover and stir occasionally, making sure the spices don't catch on the bottom of the pan and burn.

When the potatoes are tender, drain them well and return them to the saucepan. Using a sharp knife, chop the potatoes in the pan into bite-sized pieces. Add the potatoes to the sauté pan with the cauliflower and stir for 30 seconds–1 minute so they get coated in spices.

Add the onion masala, the remaining ginger, the remaining green chilli and lemon juice to taste, then stir for 30 seconds to blend the ingredients. Stir in the garam masala and about three-quarters of the chopped coriander and continue stirring over a medium-high heat so any leftover liquid evaporates. Make sure none of the ingredients catch on the bottom of the pan and burn; you really have to watch closely.

Adjust the seasoning with salt, if necessary, and sprinkle with the remaining chopped coriander before serving.

CAULIFLOWER AND CARROT CURRY

Gobi Gajar

This dish really reminds me of home and where my family comes from. It is a recipe inspired by the Tibetans who come and cook wonderful Himalayan cuisine in the highlands of Punjab and Himanchal.

SERVES 4 AS A SHARING DISH

4 garlic cloves
2 carrots
½ head of cauliflower, about 400g
½ head of broccoli, about 200g
2 tablespoons vegetable oil
1 teaspoon dried chilli flakes
1 teaspoon ground turmeric
2 tablespoons light soy sauce, or
   to taste

Assemble all the ingredients and equipment before you begin. You need a large sauté or frying pan with a lid.

Peel and thinly slice the garlic cloves. Peel the carrots, then trim both ends from each and thinly slice. Cut the piece of cauliflower in half and discard the leaves, then thinly slice. Cut the broccoli into florets, then thinly slice the florets.

Heat the vegetable oil over a high heat in the pan. Add the garlic and chilli flakes and stir around to flavour the oil. Pull the pan off the heat and stir in the carrots, cauliflower and broccoli. Return the pan to the heat and stir-fry for 2 minutes.

Cover the pan, reduce the heat to low and leave the vegetables to cook for 8 minutes, stirring once.

Stir in the turmeric and soy sauce and stir for 2–3 minutes until all the vegetables are tender, but still holding their shapes. Adjust the seasoning with extra soy sauce, if necessary.

SOUR CAULIFLOWER AND POTATOES

Khatti Aloo Gobi

From Rajisthan, this simple side dish is particularly good served alongside dal. If you'd like it as a vegetarian main course, simply double the quantities.

SERVES 4 AS A SHARING DISH

5 well-scrubbed new potatoes (see Atul's tip, below)
500g cauliflower
8 black peppercorns
1 long thin green chilli
2.5cm piece of fresh ginger
2 tablespoons vegetable oil
½ teaspoon cumin seeds
2 tablespoons passata
1½ teaspoons ground coriander
1 teaspoon dried fenugreek leaf powder
½ teaspoon red chilli powder, or to taste
½ teaspoon mango powder (*amchur*), or lemon juice
150ml water, as needed
1 lemon
fresh coriander leaves
sea salt

Bring a large covered saucepan of salted water to the boil and assemble all the ingredients and other equipment before you begin. You also need a large sauté or frying pan with a lid.

Get the potatoes cooking as quickly as possible. Quarter each potato lengthways, dropping the pieces into the boiling water as you cut. Be careful the water doesn't splash you as you add the potatoes. Cover the pan and return the water to the boil, then boil, uncovered, for 8 minutes, or until the potatoes are not quite tender.

Meanwhile, cut the cauliflower into bite-sized florets. Crush the peppercorns with the back of a wooden spoon. Remove the stalk from the green chilli, if necessary, then finely chop the chilli. Peel and finely chop the ginger.

Heat the vegetable oil over a medium-high heat in the sauté pan. Add the green chilli, ginger and cumin seeds, and stir until the seeds crackle. Add the passata and continue stirring for 30 seconds.

Add the crushed peppercorns, ground coriander, fenugreek leaf powder, chilli powder and mango powder, and stir for 30 seconds to cook the spices. Watch closely so they do not burn. (If you are substituting lemon juice for the mango powder, increase the amount of lemon juice added later to 3 tablespoons.)

Add the cauliflower florets and season with salt, stirring to coat the florets in the spicy tomato mixture. Stir in 125ml of the water, then cover the pan and leave the cauliflower to steam-cook while the potatoes finish cooking.

Drain the potatoes and add them to the cauliflower. Re-cover the pan and leave over a medium heat for 10 minutes, or until the cauliflower and potatoes are both tender. Check occasionally and add extra water, if needed, to avoid the spices burning, but do not add so much water that the cauliflower becomes mushy.

While the cauliflower finishes cooking, squeeze 2½ tablespoons of lemon juice. Rinse and chop enough coriander leaves to make about 2 tablespoons.

Uncover the pan and leave any excess liquid to bubble away. Stir in the lemon juice. Adjust the seasoning, if necessary, with salt, then sprinkle with the chopped coriander just before serving.

Atul's time-saving tip
To save time, I buy new potatoes that are well scrubbed, ready to boil. And I would never consider peeling them.

BENGALI CAULIFLOWER AND POTATOES

Panch Phoron Gobi Aloo

Here's another variation of the curry house favourite, *gobi aloo*. This is from the coastal region of Bengal, and you might never have had this classic combination with pickling spices and final finish of fresh ginger. I think this makes a great vegetarian main course, served with parathas and rice, but it's also good served alongside just about any roast meat, adding a bit of spice to a traditional Sunday lunch.

SERVES 4

12 well-scrubbed small new
   potatoes (see Atul's tip, below)
2 thin short green chillies
2 garlic cloves
2 tablespoons mustard oil
1¼ teaspoons panch phoron
2 teaspoons ground coriander
½ teaspoon red chilli powder, or
   to taste
½ teaspoon ground turmeric
425ml water
½ head of cauliflower, about 400g
1 lemon
2cm piece of fresh ginger
fresh coriander leaves
sea salt

Assemble all the ingredients and equipment before you begin. You need a large sauté or frying pan with a lid.

Quarter the new potatoes lengthways. Remove the stalks from the green chillies, if necessary, then halve the chillies lengthways. Peel and thinly slice the garlic cloves.

Heat the mustard oil over a medium-high heat in the pan. Add the garlic and stir around to flavour the oil – it doesn't need to colour. Add the green chillies and the panch phoron and stir until the seeds crackle.

Add the potatoes, ground coriander, chilli powder and turmeric. Season with salt and stir for 30 seconds to cook the spices and so the potatoes get coated. Watch closely so the spices do not burn.

Stir in the water and bring to the boil. Lower the heat to medium, cover the pan and leave the potatoes to bubble for 12 minutes, or until they are three-quarters cooked.

Meanwhile, cut the cauliflower into small bite-sized florets, discarding the outer leaves and core. Squeeze 1 tablespoon of lemon juice. Peel and finely chop the ginger. Rinse and chop enough coriander to make about 1½ tablespoons. Set all these ingredients aside separately.

When the potatoes are almost cooked, stir in the cauliflower florets and cook over a high heat for 6 minutes, stirring occasionally, until the potatoes and cauliflower are both tender, but the cauliflower is still holding its shape.

Stir in the lemon juice, 1 tablespoon of the ginger and 1 tablespoon of the chopped coriander, and adjust the seasoning with salt, if necessary. Sprinkle with the remaining ginger and coriander just before serving.

Atul's time-saving tip
I buy well-scrubbed small new potatoes when cooking this dish, so all I have to do is quarter them. If your potatoes are larger, however, cut the potatoes into 1cm dice so they cook quickly.

CABBAGE CURRY

Muttakos Kolambu

This is one of the recipes I had never actually made before I started developing recipes for this book. They all come from a collection of different food memories from different places, and this Tamil Nadu recipe is evocative of my time in southern India. I still remember seeing grandmothers sitting on the rickety chairs all over the south, wielding the knives like samurais as they cut vegetables. To be honest, I used to laugh looking at the way they could handle knives with their years of experience. Now, however, as I did all the chopping for this recipe, I'm beginning to admire them.

I think it's quite interesting that the spice powder and the tomatoes in this recipe are similar to what is often used in chicken curries. This is to satisfy a longing for meat when meat-eaters temporarily become vegetarian during religious festivals, which can last for up to a month.

SERVES 4 AS A SHARING DISH

250g white cabbage
2 long thin green chillies
2 tablespoons coconut oil
1 teaspoon black mustard seeds
10 fresh or dried curry leaves
2 tablespoons Onion Paste
    (page 218)
1 teaspoon ground turmeric
5 tablespoons canned chopped
    tomatoes
fresh coriander leaves
sea salt

For the spice powder
1 large dried red chilli
1 tablespoon coriander seeds
1 teaspoon fennel seeds
1 teaspoon white poppy seeds

Assemble all the ingredients and equipment before you begin. You need a non-stick pan for toasting the spices, a spice grinder and a wok with a cover or a large sauté or frying pan with a lid.

First prepare the spice powder. Put the chilli into the dry non-stick pan over a high heat. Add the coriander and fennel and poppy seeds and stir until the spices are aromatic. It should smell really beautiful, but watch closely so that the chilli doesn't burn before the spices are toasted. Tip the chilli and seeds into the spice grinder and grind until a fine powder forms. Set aside.

To prepare the cabbage, remove any discoloured outer leaves, cut out any piece of core and finely shred the leaves. Remove the stalks from the green chillies, if necessary, then cut the chillies in half lengthways.

Melt the coconut oil over a medium-high heat in the wok. Add the mustard seeds and stir until they pop. Add the green chillies, curry leaves and onion paste, and stir for 30 seconds.

Add the cabbage to the wok, then stir in the spice powder and the turmeric. Season with salt, turn up the heat and stir for 30 seconds to cook the turmeric and to distribute the ground spices through the cabbage. Stir in the tomatoes just as the cabbage starts to wilt.

Cover the wok, turn the heat to medium and leave the cabbage to steam-cook, stirring occasionally, for 7 minutes, or until it is tender.

Meanwhile, rinse and chop enough coriander leaves to make about 2 tablespoons.

Adjust the seasoning with salt, if necessary, and stir the chopped coriander through the cabbage just before serving.

CABBAGE, KERALA STYLE

Muttakos Thoran

I had such an enjoyable time developing this recipe. I used every cabbage available, and the final colour was beautiful, especially with the red cabbage I included. Use whatever varieties you can get hold of – even all white or Savoy cabbages work just fine – as long as the total weight comes to about 500g. I think this is a particularly good way to use up fresh cabbage left over from another recipe.

I've called this 'Kerala style' purely to distinguish it from cabbage dishes from north India, and you'll find similar preparations all over southern India. It's a very basic, common dish made in many households on a daily basis. It is also somewhat unique in that some of the spices are sautéed and some are added raw – the cumin seeds, for example, are steamed in the residual moisture while the cabbage cooks. I've chosen to sauté the garlic, but I know some people just add it raw. This is also one of the few recipes where I add curry leaves straight into the oil.

SERVES 4 AS A SHARING DISH

150g red cabbage
150g Savoy cabbage
150g white cabbage
3 large Chinese cabbage leaves
5 garlic cloves
2 long thin green chillies
2 shallots
2 tablespoons coconut oil
2 teaspoons black mustard seeds
15 fresh or dried curry leaves
1 teaspoon cumin seeds
4 heaped tablespoons frozen grated
   coconut, plus extra to garnish
sea salt

Assemble all the ingredients and equipment before you begin. You need a large wok with a cover or a large sauté or frying pan with a lid.

Remove and discard the outer leaves from all the cabbages you are using and cut out any pieces of core, then thinly slice each. Rinse the Chinese cabbage leaves, then remove the thick central stalks and thinly slice.

Peel and slice the garlic cloves. Remove the stalks from the green chillies, if necessary, then cut each chilli in half lengthways. Peel, halve and slice the shallots.

Melt the coconut oil over a medium-high heat in the wok. Add the mustard seeds and stir until they pop. Add the garlic, green chillies and curry leaves, and stir them around to flavour the oil.

Add all the cabbages, the shallots, cumin seeds and 1 teaspoon of salt, and stir-fry until the ingredients are mixed together.

Turn the heat to low. Stir in the frozen coconut, then cover and leave for about 10 minutes, stirring occasionally, until the Chinese leaves are wilted and the cabbages are tender, but still with a little crunch. The cabbages are added all at once, so they will have different textures, but just keep checking so they don't over-cook.

Meanwhile, set aside a small amount of grated coconut to thaw, ready to use as a garnish.

Adjust the seasoning with salt, if necessary. Sprinkle with extra grated coconut just before serving – it will finish thawing in the residual heat if it hasn't already done so.

SQUASH AND PEANUT CURRY

Kadoo Shengdana

Inspired by the cooking of Vietnam and Thailand, this is a very different curry from the ones I normally make. It includes many of the same ingredients I cook with every day – chillies, fresh coriander, garlic and ginger – but with a very different flavour. It's amazing how a small change can make such a difference. An authentic South-East Asian curry would contain fish sauce, but I've decided against including it so this remains vegetarian.

SERVES 4 AS A SHARING DISH

2½ tablespoons smooth
   peanut butter
400ml hot water
1 lime
1–2 tablespoons light soy sauce,
   to taste
300g butternut squash (see Atul's
   tip, below)
5cm piece of fresh ginger
3 garlic cloves
1 long thin green chilli
½ red onion
fresh coriander sprigs
2 tablespoons vegetable oil
250ml coconut milk

Assemble all the ingredients and equipment before you begin. You need a whisk, a large bowl, a fine grater and a large sauté or frying pan.

Whisk the peanut butter and 100ml of the water together in the bowl. Grate in the zest and squeeze in the juice of the lime and whisk in 1 tablespoon of the soy sauce. Set aside.

Peel, quarter and cut the squash into 0.5cm slices. Peel and finely chop the ginger. Peel and thinly slice the garlic cloves. Remove the stalk from the green chilli, if necessary, then finely chop the chilli. Halve, peel and thinly slice the onion. Rinse the coriander sprigs and separate the stalks and leaves. Finely chop the stalks and chop enough leaves to make about 1 tablespoon, then set aside separately.

Heat the vegetable oil over a medium-high heat in the pan. Add the onion and stir for about 1 minute. Add the ginger, green chilli, coriander stalks and garlic, and continue stirring until the onion is softened, but not coloured.

Stir in the squash, coating it with the flavourings. Add the coconut milk and the remaining 300ml water, stirring until the mixture comes to the boil. Re-whisk the peanut butter mixture, then add it to the pan, stirring to dissolve the peanut butter. Leave the mixture to gently boil and reduce for about 15 minutes, stirring occasionally, until the squash is tender. Check occasionally that the mixture isn't sticking on the bottom of the pan.

Stir in half the chopped coriander leaves and adjust the seasoning with the remaining soy sauce, if necessary. Sprinkle with the remaining chopped coriander leaves just before serving.

Atul's time-saving tip
Use the neck end of the squash so you don't have to spend time removing the seeds.

SQUASH AND LENTILS

Mattanna Kootu

Kootu is a south Indian vegetable preparation that always includes lentils. I'm making it here with squash, but you can also use cabbage, cauliflower or pumpkin. The thing to remember is not to over-cook the vegetable, because you want it holding its shape. I like using butternut squash because it never breaks down totally.

SERVES 4 AS A SHARING DISH

75g split yellow mung dal
   (*moong daal*)
750g butternut squash
1 tablespoon coconut oil
¼ teaspoon ground asafoetida
1 teaspoon cumin seeds
1 teaspoon black mustard seeds
10 fresh or dried curry leaves
1 large dried red chilli
½ teaspoon ground turmeric
about 200ml water, as needed
sea salt

For the coconut paste
4 tablespoons frozen grated coconut,
   plus extra to garnish
1 large dried red chilli
½ teaspoon cumin seeds

Bring a large covered saucepan of water to the boil and assemble all the ingredients and other equipment before you begin. You also need a colander or sieve, a spice grinder and a large sauté or frying pan with a lid.

Rinse the lentils in the colander, then add them to the boiling water. Return the water to the boil and boil the lentils, uncovered, for 15 minutes, or until they are tender. Drain well and set aside.

Meanwhile, make the coconut paste. Add the frozen coconut to a spice grinder, and set aside a little extra to thaw for the garnish. Tear the dried chilli into the spice grinder, add the cumin seeds and grind until a coarse paste forms. Set aside.

Peel the butternut squash, then cut it in half and scrape out the seeds. Cut the flesh into 2cm cubes, trying to keep them a uniform size.

Melt the coconut oil over a medium-high heat in the sauté pan. Add the asafoetida and stir until it sizzles. Add the cumin and mustard seeds and stir until the cumin seeds crackle and the mustard seeds pop. Add the curry leaves and dried chilli and stir them around to flavour the oil. Watch closely so nothing burns.

Add the squash pieces and the turmeric to the pan. Season with salt and stir for 30 seconds to cook the turmeric. Add half the water – stand well back when you add the water, because there will be lots of steam – and cover the pan. Leave the squash to steam-cook for 15 minutes, or until tender. Check occasionally and stir in the extra water if the squash or spices are sticking to the bottom of the pan.

Uncover the pan, turn up the heat and let any excess water evaporate. Add the spice paste and lentils and stir together to reheat the lentils. Adjust the seasoning with salt, if necessary. Sprinkle with the coconut for serving – it will finish thawing in the residual heat if it hasn't already done so.

SPICED MARROW WITH MUSTARD SEEDS

Sarson Ki Lauki

We absolutely adore this in *casa* Kochhar, and amazingly enough even my children will clean their plates when this dish is on the menu. I leave the peel on the marrow in this recipe from the Gujarat region simply because I quite like it, but feel free to take it off if you'd rather.

SERVES 4 AS A SHARING DISH

1 large marrow
1 tablespoon ground coriander
1 teaspoon red chilli powder, or
   to taste
1 teaspoon ground turmeric
2 tablespoons mustard oil
¼ teaspoon ground asafoetida
1 dried bay leaf
1 large dried red chilli
2 teaspoons black mustard seeds
1 teaspoon cumin seeds
1 teaspoon fenugreek seeds
1 tablespoon mango powder
   (*amchur*), or lemon juice
2 tablespoons Greek-style yogurt
4 tablespoons water
sea salt

Assemble all the ingredients and equipment before you begin. You need a small bowl and a large sauté or frying pan with a lid.

Rinse the marrow, then cut off the ends. Halve it crossways, then quarter each half and scrape out the seeds. Cut the flesh into bite-sized pieces.

Put the ground coriander, chilli powder and turmeric in a small bowl, and mix together. Set aside.

Melt the mustard oil over a medium-high heat in the pan. Add the asafoetida and stir until it sizzles. Add the bay leaf and the dried chilli and stir them around to flavour the oil. Add the mustard, cumin and fenugreek seeds, and stir until the mustard seeds pop, the cumin seeds crackle and the fenugreek seeds turn darker. It is very important that the seeds are well cooked at this point, but watch closely so they don't burn.

Add the marrow to the pan. Season with salt and stir so all the pieces are coated in the oil and spices. Add the mango powder and stir for 30 seconds. (If you're substituting lemon juice for the mango powder, add it at the end when the marrow is tender.) Add the ground spice mixture and cook for 30 seconds to cook the spices. Watch closely so they do not burn.

Stir in the yogurt, which adds a creaminess that coats the marrow with spices and a little moisture to prevent the spices from burning. Stir in the water, cover the pan, turn the heat to medium-low and leave the marrow to cook for about 15 minutes, stirring occasionally, until it is tender. Adjust the seasoning with salt, if necessary, and serve.

SPICED COURGETTES AND ONIONS

Turai Ka Salan

I love simple dishes like this – they have so much to offer. This is, however, a very spicy, hot dish. It is adaptable for all tastes, though. I've specified mild green chillies in this recipe, but you can de-seed them to tone down the spiciness even more, or replace them with small red chillies for intense heat.

SERVES 4 AS A SHARING DISH

2 long thin green chillies
2 large courgettes
2 onions
2 tablespoons vegetable oil
1 teaspoon cumin seeds
1 teaspoon black mustard seeds
10 fresh or dried curry leaves
½ teaspoon red chilli powder, or
   to taste
½ teaspoon ground turmeric
4 tablespoons water
fresh coriander leaves
sea salt

Assemble all the ingredients and equipment before you begin. You need a large sauté or frying pan with a lid.

Remove the stalks from the green chillies, if necessary, then thinly slice the chillies. Cut off both ends from the courgettes, then cut into slices about 0.5cm thick. Peel, halve and slice the onions.

Heat the vegetable oil over a medium-high heat in the pan. Add the cumin and mustard seeds and stir until the cumin seeds crackle and the mustard seeds pop. Add the green chillies, onions and curry leaves with a pinch of salt and stir until the onions are softened, but not coloured.

Add the courgettes, chilli powder and turmeric, and stir for 30 seconds to cook the spices. Watch closely so they do not burn. Stir in the water. Cover the pan and leave the courgettes to steam-cook, stirring occasionally to make sure nothing sticks to the bottom of the pan, for 10 minutes, or until they are tender.

Meanwhile, rinse and chop enough coriander leaves to make about 2 tablespoons.

Adjust the seasoning with salt, if necessary, and sprinkle with the chopped coriander before serving.

SPICED FRUITY POTATOES

Hing Aloo Kishmish

I don't use a lot of ghee in my cooking. I'm not a big fan, but occasionally classic recipes like this sweet, sour and savoury dish just demand it – and the aroma that comes from the pan while everything is cooking is unbeatable. If you want to keep this strictly vegetarian, however, use vegetable oil instead.

The sour note comes from ground pomegranate seeds, which you can buy in powder form from Indian food shops. It doesn't need cooking, so I add it towards the end, not with the other ground spices. If you can't find the powder, substitute Middle Eastern sumac. An alternative to pomegranate powder or sumac would be to use prepared pomegranate seeds which can be found in supermarkets or Middle Eastern food shops, or remove the seeds from half a pomegranate, remove the pith and scatter them over the potatoes.

SERVES 4 AS A SHARING DISH

12 well-scrubbed new potatoes (see Atul's tip, page 29)
2 tablespoons raisins
1 long thin green chilli
fresh coriander leaves
2.5cm piece of fresh ginger
12 seedless green grapes
2 tablespoons ghee
½ teaspoon ground asafoetida
1 teaspoon cumin seeds
½ teaspoon red chilli powder
½ teaspoon ground turmeric
45g prepared pomegranate seeds
2 teaspoons pomegranate seed powder (*anardana*), or sumac
sea salt

Bring a covered saucepan of salted water to the boil and assemble all the ingredients and other equipment before you begin. You also need a small bowl, a large sauté or frying pan and a slotted spoon.

Get the potatoes cooking as soon as possible. Cut each potato into slices about 1cm thick, dropping the slices into the boiling water as you cut. Be careful that the water doesn't splash you as you add the potatoes. Re-cover the pan and return the water to the boil, then boil, uncovered, for 12–15 minutes until the slices are tender. Drain well and set aside.

Meanwhile, prepare the remaining ingredients. Put the raisins in the small bowl and cover with hot water. Remove the stalk from the green chilli, if necessary, then thinly slice the chilli. Rinse and chop enough coriander leaves to make about 2 tablespoons. Peel and finely chop the ginger. Rinse the grapes.

Melt the ghee over a medium-high heat in the sauté pan. Add the asafoetida and stir until it sizzles. Add the cumin seeds and stir until they crackle. Add the green chilli and ginger and continue stirring for about 30 seconds to flavour the ghee.

Add the potatoes to the pan. Season with salt and stir the potatoes around the pan to coat them in ghee and spices. Add the red chilli powder and turmeric and continue stirring for 30 seconds to cook the spices. Watch closely so they do not burn.

Use a slotted spoon to transfer the raisins to the pan, then add about 2 tablespoons of their soaking liquid. Stir in the grapes and pomegranate seeds. Increase the heat to high and stir for 30 seconds–1 minute to soften the grapes.

Stir in the pomegranate powder and chopped coriander and leave for 30 seconds for the flavours to blend. Adjust the seasoning with salt, if necessary and then serve.

SPICED POTATOES AND COCONUT

Urulai Sukka

Sukka means 'dry', so less liquid is added to this recipe compared with others. If you leave any leftovers in the fridge, however, you will have to add a bit more liquid while reheating, because the coconut will have absorbed what liquid there is.

SERVES 4 AS A SHARING DISH

500g well-scrubbed small new
  potatoes (see Atul's tip, page 31)
1 tablespoon coconut oil
1 teaspoon black mustard seeds
10 fresh or dried curry leaves
200ml water
½ teaspoon ground turmeric
1 tablespoon jaggery or palm sugar
½ lime
sea salt

For the spice paste

1½ tablespoons coconut oil
3 large dried red chillies
3 tablespoons toor lentils (*toor daal*)
1 tablespoon coriander seeds
¼ teaspoon fenugreek seeds
100g frozen grated coconut
125ml water
4 tablespoons Tamarind Liquid
  (page 223)

Bring a large covered saucepan of salted water to the boil and assemble all the ingredients and other equipment before you begin. You also need a non-stick pan for toasting the chillies, lentils and spices, a food processor fitted with a chopping blade and a large sauté or frying pan.

Get the potatoes cooking as quickly as possible. Halve the potatoes, adding them to the boiling water as you cut. Be careful that the water doesn't splash you as you add them to the pan. Re-cover the pan and return the water to the boil. Once boiling, uncover and boil the potatoes for 18 minutes, or until tender. Drain well and set aside.

Meanwhile, make the spice paste. Melt the 1½ tablespoons of coconut oil in the non-stick pan over a medium-high heat. Add the dried chillies, lentils and coriander and fenugreek seeds, and stir until the coriander seeds crackle and the lentils are golden brown and crisp. Turn the heat down as the lentils toast so they don't burn. Transfer all these ingredients to the food processor and set aside. Wipe out the pan, if necessary.

Toast the coconut over a low heat in the wiped pan. Add it to the food processor with the water and tamarind liquid, then blitz, scraping down the sides of the bowl as necessary, until a coarse, chunky paste forms. Set aside.

Melt the 1 tablespoon of coconut oil over a medium-high heat in the sauté pan. Add the mustard seeds and stir until they pop. Turn the heat down, add the spice paste and curry leaves and stir together.

Add the water and bring to the boil. Add the turmeric, season with salt and continue stirring for 5 minutes to cook the lentils in the spice paste. Watch closely so the mixture doesn't catch and burn.

Add the drained potatoes and stir until they are coated with the spice paste. Crumble over the palm sugar and squeeze in the lime juice to taste, then mix well. Adjust the seasoning with salt, if necessary, and serve.

SPICED CARROTS AND PARSNIPS

Rang Birangi Gajar

Simple and straightforward, this is an old-fashioned, home-style recipe. I hesitated about including such a simple recipe as this, but it tastes so good it had to be included. I've always loved the flavour of parsnips, but they aren't a natural vegetable to India and so they are imported. I could have complicated this by adding nuts, but the joy of this recipe is that it's just so simple as it is.

Of course you can make this with all orange carrots, but I like to use a selection of multi-coloured heritage baby carrots as they look so beautiful.

SERVES 4 AS A SHARING DISH

300g baby carrots – leave them whole with a little of the green tops attached
2 garlic cloves
1 large parsnip
1 small onion
1 long thin green chilli
fresh coriander leaves
1 tablespoon coconut oil
1 teaspoon cumin seeds
½ teaspoon black mustard seeds
½ lime
1 teaspoon ground coriander
¼ teaspoon red chilli powder, or to taste
sea salt

Bring a large covered saucepan of water to the boil and assemble all the ingredients and other equipment before you begin. You also need a large sauté or frying pan.

I never peel baby carrots, but if you want them peeled it's best to do that after they have boiled, when the peels can be easily – and quickly – pulled off. Just give the carrots a good scrub now and set aside.

Peel and thinly slice the garlic cloves. Peel the parsnip, then quarter it lengthways and remove the core, if necessary. Cut the thicker pieces again lengthways so they are about the same thickness as the carrots. Peel, halve and finely chop the onion. Remove the stalk from the green chilli, if necessary, then cut the chilli in half lengthways. Rinse and finely chop enough coriander leaves to make about 1 tablespoon.

Add the parsnips and ½ teaspoon of salt to the boiling water, re-cover the pan and boil for 1 minute. Add the baby carrots, return the water to the boil and leave to boil, uncovered, for 4½ minutes, or until the vegetables are tender-crisp.

Meanwhile, melt the coconut oil over a medium-high heat in the pan. Add the cumin and mustard seeds and garlic and stir until the cumin seeds crackle and the mustard seeds pop. Add the onion with a pinch of salt and continue stirring until it is softened, but not coloured. Stir in the green chillies. Turn the heat to low and leave the onion to gently continue cooking while you tend to the parsnips and carrots.

When the parsnip pieces and carrots are tender, drain them and run them under cold water to stop them cooking. Cut any of the thick carrots in half lengthways. If you want peeled carrots, now is the time to lift off the thin peels.

Add the parsnips and carrots to the onions with a pinch of salt and stir together. Squeeze in lime juice to taste, then add the ground coriander and chilli powder and stir for 30 seconds to cook the spices. Adjust the

seasoning with salt, if necessary. Sprinkle with the chopped coriander just before serving.

Atul's time-saving tip
Adding a pinch of salt when you sauté the onions draws out their moisture, helping them soften quicker.

SPICED ROAST POTATOES

Achari Aloo

Normally I would suggest 500g potatoes to serve 4 people, but my assistant reminded me how much everyone just loves roast potatoes, so you might as well make lots. And, even if you don't want to roast all the potatoes, I don't think you can ever go wrong having boiled potatoes in the fridge. As every Indian cook will tell you, you are halfway towards making a quick Indian meal when you have cooked potatoes in the fridge.

If you do decide to just use 500g potatoes for four portions of this recipe, however, reduce all the other ingredients by half as well.

SERVES 8
(see the recipe introduction)

1kg well-scrubbed small new
  potatoes (see Atul's tip, page 29)
1 tablespoon mango powder
  (*amchur*), or lemon juice
1 teaspoon ground turmeric
½ teaspoon red chilli powder, or
  to taste
6 tablespoons vegetable oil
fresh coriander leaves
1 large dried red chilli
½ teaspoon cumin seeds
½ teaspoon black mustard seeds
½ teaspoon onion seeds
4 teaspoons white wine vinegar
1 teaspoon caster sugar
½ teaspoon garam masala
sea salt

Preheat the oven to 220ºC/Fan 200ºC/Gas Mark 7, bring a large covered saucepan of salted water to the boil and assemble all the ingredients and other equipment before you begin. You also need a large sieve or colander, a large bowl, a roasting tray and a large sauté or frying pan.

Get the potatoes cooking as quickly as possible. Halve the potatoes, adding the halves to the boiling water as you cut. Be careful that the water doesn't splash you as you add them to the pan. Re-cover the pan and return the water to the boil, then boil the potatoes for 8 minutes.

Add the roasting tray to the oven to heat up once the potatoes have boiled for 5 minutes.

Meanwhile, mix the mango powder, turmeric and chilli powder in the bowl. (If you're substituting lemon juice for the mango powder, add it in the final step with the vinegar.) Stir in 4 tablespoons of the vegetable oil and season with salt. Chop enough coriander leaves to make about 2 tablespoons. Set both aside separately.

Drain the potatoes well, shaking off as much water as possible. Add them to the spice mixture in the bowl and mix together so the potatoes are well coated. Tip the potatoes into the hot roasting tray in a single layer. Place the tray in the oven and roast the potatoes for 10 minutes, stirring occasionally, or until tender.

After 5 minutes, heat the remaining 2 tablespoons of oil over a medium-high heat in the sauté pan. Add the dried chilli and cumin, mustard and onion seeds, and stir until the cumin and onion seeds crackle and the mustard seeds pop. Watch closely so the spices do not burn.

Tip the roasted potatoes into the sauté pan and stir for 2 minutes, or until they are browned. Add the chopped coriander, vinegar, sugar and garam masala, and stir for a further 30 seconds. Adjust the seasoning with salt, if necessary and then serve.

SPICED GRATED BEETROOT AND COCONUT

Birrutt Thuran

I'm suggesting starting with raw beetroot for the recipe, but if you find boiled ones in the supermarket or at a green grocer's buy them (just avoid the ones in vinegar). If you want real bang for your buck, however, then I recommend the raw ones. Yes, they do take longer to cook, but I think the earthy flavour of the beetroot really comes through. Beetroot isn't a very common vegetable for vegetarian main or sharing dishes in India, as it's more commonly treated as a salad ingredient. Nevertheless, I think it works well in this dish from southern India.

When you're cooking cumin and mustard seeds in any recipe, it's essential they cook until the cumin seeds crackle and the mustard seeds pop, otherwise they will taste raw, two flavours I particularly do not like.

SERVES 4 AS A SHARING DISH

2 large raw beetroots, about 450g
 total weight
2.5cm piece of fresh ginger
5 shallots
2 long thin green chillies
1 heaped tablespoon coconut oil
1 large dried red chilli
1 tablespoon black mustard seeds
½ teaspoon cumin seeds
12 fresh or dried curry leaves
2 teaspoons ground coriander
1 teaspoon garam masala
½ teaspoon ground turmeric
½ teaspoon chilli powder, or to taste
3 tablespoons grated frozen coconut,
 plus extra to garnish
sea salt

Assemble all the ingredients and equipment before you begin. You need a food processor fitted with a fine grating blade or a fine grater and a sauté or frying pan with a lid.

Peel the beetroots, then quarter them and finely grate them in the food processor. Set aside.

Peel and finely chop the ginger. Peel, halve and thinly slice the shallots. Remove the stalks from the green chillies, if necessary, then slice the chillies in half lengthways.

Melt the coconut oil over a medium-high heat in the pan. Add the dried chilli and mustard and cumin seeds and stir until the mustard seeds pop and the cumin seeds crackle. Add the shallots and green chillies and stir until the shallots soften, but don't colour.

Lower the heat to medium. Stir in the grated beetroot and the ginger. Add the curry leaves, ground coriander, garam masala, turmeric, chilli powder and ½ teaspoon of salt, and stir for 30 seconds to incorporate all the spices and cook them. Watch closely so they do not burn.

Cover the pan and leave the beetroot to cook for 2–3 minutes until it is tender. Stir in the frozen coconut and warm through. When you take the coconut out of the freezer set aside a little extra to use as a garnish.

Adjust the seasoning with salt, if necessary. Sprinkle with extra coconut just before serving – it will thaw in the residual heat.

Atul's time-saving tip

I've suggested using a food processor for grating the beetroot to save time, but it also prevents dyeing your hands red. That's something I hate.

MIXED ONION STIR-FRY

Pyaz ki Tarkari

This is a quick stir-fry recipe that is very delicious, basically, because onions have so many flavours. They feature big in Indian cooking, and without onions there would not be any life in India, in my opinion ... well, maybe there would be life, but it wouldn't be as good. I don't think it's important to be too dogmatic about the onions you use, just make sure you have a variety. You can also include leeks if you happen to have some, and they will add a new dimension to this.

Onions take up a lot of oil as they cook, but then they release it again, which is why you find what looks like a litre of oil floating on curries in many Indian restaurants. I think it's painful to look at those curries.

SERVES 4–6 AS A SHARING DISH

2 large white onions
1 red onion
1 yellow (ordinary) onion
1 bunch of spring onions
3 tablespoons vegetable oil
1 teaspoon cumin seeds
1 teaspoon onion seeds
1 teaspoon red chilli powder, or
  to taste
1 teaspoon ground turmeric
2 teaspoons Ginger–Garlic Paste
  (page 220)
4 tablespoons water
fresh coriander leaves
sea salt

Assemble all the ingredients and equipment before you begin. You need a large sauté or frying pan or a wok.

Peel, halve and thickly slice the white, red and yellow onions. Trim the roots from the spring onions, then cut into lengths that include the white parts and about 4cm of the green stalks. Do not discard the remaining green stalks, because they are added towards the end of the recipe.

Heat the vegetable oil over a medium-high heat in the pan. Add the cumin and onion seeds and stir until the cumin seeds crackle and onion seeds pop. Reduce the heat to medium, add all the onions, including the chopped spring onions, the chilli powder and turmeric, and stir for 30 seconds–1 minute to cook the spices. Add the ginger-garlic paste and stir for a further 30 seconds. Watch closely so nothing burns.

Stir in the water. Season with salt and continue stirring, scraping in any caramelised bits from the bottom of the pan. Leave to simmer, uncovered and stirring occasionally, for about 10 minutes or until the onions are just softened.

Meanwhile, chop the reserved spring onion stalks into 5cm strips. Rinse and chop enough coriander leaves to make about 1 tablespoon.

When the onions are tender, add the spring onion strips and stir for about 2 minutes until they are tender. Adjust the seasoning with salt, if necessary, and sprinkle with the chopped coriander before serving.

TURNIP CURRY

Shalijam Kori

Turnips are one of those vegetables that absorb the flavours they are cooked with, making them a natural for quick cooking. It never fails to amaze me how something so basic and simple becomes so exciting and satisfying. The transformation begins when the bay leaves and cinnamon stick are added to the ghee. I like the sweetness of cinnamon in curries, and typical of Bengali recipes this also includes a small amount of sugar.

As a child I decided I hated turnips, but my mother had a very different view. She never got angry with me, she simply said, 'Fine, suit yourself, because that's the only vegetable we have today.' If I liked them I could eat them, if I didn't like them I could still eat them, and if I didn't want to do that there was always bed. So, as a young, arrogant teenager, I went off to bed. In the morning, guess what there was to go with the flat breads? Yes, you've got it – turnips. So I went off to school with an empty stomach. When I got home there were turnips again ... and *finally* I started eating turnips. The moral of the story – don't mess with your mum!

SERVES 4 AS A SHARING DISH

4 large turnips, about 600g
   total weight
1½ teaspoons ground turmeric
1 tablespoon ghee
1 tablespoon vegetable oil
2 dried bay leaves
1 cinnamon stick
1 teaspoon cumin seeds
3 tablespoons Onion Paste
   (page 218)
6 tablespoons passata
2 teaspoons ground coriander
1 teaspoon sugar
½ teaspoon red chilli powder, or
   to taste
375ml water, or as needed
fresh coriander leaves
½ teaspoon garam masala
sea salt

Bring a large covered saucepan of water to the boil and assemble all the ingredients and other equipment before you begin. You also need a large sauté or frying pan with a lid and a colander or sieve.

Get the turnips cooking as soon as possible. Rinse the turnips well and decide if you need to scrub or peel them, then cut off the tops and tails and cut them into wedges. My turnips looked so beautiful when I was testing this recipe that I didn't bother with scrubbing or peeling, but that isn't always the case. Put the wedges in the boiling water with ½ teaspoon of the turmeric. Season with salt, stir well, re-cover the pan and return the water to the boil, then boil for 7 minutes, or until the turnips are tender-crisp.

Meanwhile, melt the ghee with the vegetable oil over a medium-high heat in the pan. Add the bay leaves and cinnamon stick and stir around to flavour the ghee. Add the cumin seeds and stir until they crackle. Add the onion paste and stir it into the ghee and oil for 30 seconds.

Lower the heat to medium, add the passata, the remaining 1 teaspoon of the turmeric, the ground coriander, sugar and chilli powder. Season with salt and stir for 30 seconds to cook the spices. Watch closely so they do not burn. Stir in the water and bring to the boil.

When the turnips are almost cooked, drain and stir them into the gravy. Add extra water, if necessary, so the turnips are just submerged. Cover the pan and leave the turnips to simmer over a medium heat for 5–10 minutes until they are tender.

Meanwhile, rinse and chop enough coriander leaves to make about 2 tablespoons.

Just before serving, stir the garam masala and three-quarters of the chopped coriander into the curry. Adjust the seasoning with salt, if necessary, and garnish with the remaining chopped coriander to serve.

Atul's time-saving tip
Are you surprised to see Italian passata in the list of ingredients? You shouldn't be – I always have a jar in the cupboard for when I'm in a hurry and I use it in many of the recipes in this collection. It saves the time of peeling, de-seeding and puréeing tomatoes.

SPICED MOOLI AND TOMATOES

Mooli Iamater

I really like unusual combinations of vegetables to serve alongside lentils, and I don't think many people will have thought of cooking mooli like this. Moolis look like fat white carrots, but have a radish-like flavour, hence they are often called Indian radishes and are a popular vegetable throughout the country. You'll find moolis in Indian food shops and some large supermarkets, or labelled as daikons in South-East Asian food shops.

The spices I use here give this dish a Kashmiri flavour. I suggest a final flourish of chopped fresh ginger and fresh coriander, but if you want even more of a kick add a finely chopped green chilli.

SERVES 4 AS A SHARING DISH

1 mooli (or daikon), about 400g
4 tomatoes
2.5cm piece of fresh ginger
fresh coriander leaves
1 tablespoon vegetable oil
¼ teaspoon ground asafoetida
½ teaspoon cumin seeds
¼ teaspoon fenugreek seeds
2 teaspoons ground coriander
½ teaspoon red chilli powder, or
   to taste
½ teaspoon sugar
¼ teaspoon ground ginger
½ lemon
sea salt

Assemble all the ingredients and equipment before you begin. You need a large sauté or frying pan with a lid.

Peel and halve the mooli lengthways, then cut it into thin slices. Quarter and coarsely chop the tomatoes. Peel and finely chop the ginger. Rinse and chop enough coriander leaves to make about 3 tablespoons.

Heat the vegetable oil over a medium-high heat in the pan. Add the asafoetida and stir until it sizzles. Add the cumin and fenugreek seeds and stir until the cumin seeds crackle and the fenugreek seeds turn darker. Add the mooli and tomatoes and stir to coat them in the oil and spices. Lower the heat to medium and continue stirring occasionally for 3 minutes, or until the tomatoes start to soften.

Add the ground coriander, chilli powder, sugar and ground ginger. Season with salt and stir for 30 seconds–1 minute to cook the spices. Watch closely so they do not burn. Stir in half the chopped ginger and half the coriander leaves. Cover the pan and leave the mixture to cook for 5–8 minutes until the mooli is tender and the tomatoes have broken down.

Squeeze in 1 teaspoon of lemon juice. Cover and leave for a further 30 seconds for the flavours to blend. Adjust the seasoning with salt, if necessary.

Transfer the vegetables to a serving bowl, scraping in any brown bits from the bottom of the pan, which are quite delicious. Garnish with the remaining chopped coriander and chopped ginger.

CURRIED KOHLRABI

Ganth Gobi Ki Subji

When kohlrabi isn't available, use the long white radish called mooli or daikon and you'll get similar results.

SERVES 4 AS A SHARING DISH

400g kohlrabi
1cm piece of fresh ginger
2 tablespoons vegetable oil
¼ teaspoon ground asafoetida
2 cloves
½ teaspoon cumin seeds
¼ teaspoon fenugreek seeds
2½ teaspoons ground ginger
1 teaspoon red chilli powder, or
  to taste
1 teaspoon ground coriander
1 teaspoon garam masala
1 teaspoon ground turmeric
1 teaspoon sugar
80ml water
fresh coriander leaves
½ lemon
sea salt

Assemble all the ingredients and equipment before you begin. You need a large sauté or frying pan with a lid.

Peel the kohlrabi, then cut it into thin slices. Peel and very finely chop the ginger.

Heat the vegetable oil over a medium-high heat in the pan. Add the asafoetida and stir until it sizzles. Add the cloves and cumin and fenugreek seeds and stir until the cloves and cumin seeds crackle and the fenugreek seeds turn darker. Add the kohlrabi with a pinch of salt and stir for 2 minutes.

Add the ground ginger, chilli powder, ground coriander, garam masala, turmeric and sugar, and stir for 30 seconds to cook the spices. Watch closely so they do not burn. Add the chopped ginger and water. Reduce the heat to medium, cover the pan and leave the kohlrabi to steam-cook for 5–8 minutes until tender.

Meanwhile, rinse and chop enough coriander leaves to make about 1½ tablespoons.

Add 1 tablespoon of the chopped coriander to the pan and squeeze in 2 teaspoons of lemon juice. Stir together, re-cover the pan and leave for 30 seconds or so for the flavours to blend.

Adjust the seasoning with salt, if necessary, then sprinkle with the remaining coriander leaves before serving.

SAUTÉED MUSHROOMS

Koon Theeyal

I love cooking mushrooms, I love the combination of mushrooms and garlic and I love the sheer variety of mushrooms. When it comes to planning the menu for my chef's table at Benares, I like to use them all. I'm using wild mushrooms here, including porcini – one of my favourites – but the recipe is just as successful with any mushrooms, including cultivated ones. The more variety you use, however, the more I think you'll enjoy this dish with sourness from tamarind added at the last minute.

SERVES 4 AS A SHARING DISH

150g mixed wild mushrooms
2 garlic cloves
2 tomatoes
1 onion
2.5cm piece of fresh ginger
3½ tablespoons coconut oil
½ teaspoon black mustard seeds
20 fresh or dried curry leaves
½ teaspoon fennel seeds
1 teaspoon ground coriander
½ teaspoon red chilli powder, or
    to taste
½ teaspoon garam masala
¼ teaspoon turmeric
3 tablespoons Tamarind Liquid
    (page 223)
sea salt

Assemble all the ingredients and equipment before you begin. You need a heavy-based saucepan and a sauté or frying pan.

Wipe and trim the mushrooms, if necessary. Tear any thin mushrooms into strips and thinly slice larger or chunkier ones. Peel and thinly slice the garlic cloves. Coarsely chop the tomatoes. Peel, halve and slice the onion. Peel and finely chop the ginger.

Heat the saucepan over a medium-high heat until it is very hot. Add 2 tablespoons of the coconut oil. Add the mustard seeds and stir until they pop. Add the onion, ginger, curry leaves and fennel seeds, reduce the heat to medium, and stir until the onion is softened, but not coloured. Set aside.

Melt the remaining 1½ tablespoons of the coconut oil over a medium heat in the sauté pan. Add the garlic and stir it around to flavour the oil without letting it colour. Add all the mushrooms and stir until they start to reduce in volume. Pay close attention to make sure none of the mushrooms stick to the bottom of the pan. Add a pinch of salt, cover the pan, reduce the heat and leave the mushrooms to sweat for 2–3 minutes until they are tender.

Add the onion mixture to the mushrooms, stirring to combine all the ingredients. Add the ground coriander, chilli powder, garam masala and turmeric, and stir for 30 seconds to cook the spices. Watch closely so they do not burn. Stir in 2 tablespoons of the tamarind liquid.

Add the tomatoes and gently stir over a medium-high heat until the tomatoes just start to break down. Just before serving, stir in the remaining tamarind, for a nice tangy finish, and adjust the seasoning with salt, if necessary.

NEPALESE MUSHROOMS

Chiayou

Mushrooms have always been one of my favourite ingredients, and I love cooking them. It can be a bit labour intensive prepping mushrooms, but the good thing is that once they go in the pan they cook very quickly. A Nepalese cook might laugh at this dish, because I haven't made it as spicy hot as you would get in Nepal, but, frankly, I prefer it this way.

SERVES 4 AS A SHARING DISH

300g wild mushrooms (such as maitake, shiitake and oyster)
4 garlic cloves
2 tomatoes
1 onion
a large bunch of fresh chives
4 tablespoons vegetable oil
¼ teaspoon ground asafoetida
¼ teaspoon fenugreek seeds
1 tablespoon ground coriander
1 teaspoon red chilli powder, or to taste
1 teaspoon ground cumin
½ teaspoon ground turmeric
8 tablespoons Greek-style yogurt
sea salt

Assemble all the ingredients and equipment before you begin. You need 2 large sauté or frying pans.

Wipe and remove the stalks from the maitake and oyster mushrooms, then thinly slice the caps and stalks. Tear the shiitake mushrooms into long strips. Or trim, wipe and slice or chop whatever mushrooms you are using. Peel and roughly chop the garlic cloves. Halve the tomatoes and quarter each half. Peel, halve and slice the onion. Finely chop enough chives to make about 4 tablespoons, reserving a few chives for garnishing.

Heat 2 tablespoons of the vegetable oil over a high heat. Add the garlic and stir for 30 seconds to flavour the oil. Add the mushrooms and fry, stirring frequently, for 4–5 minutes until they are tender.

Meanwhile, heat the remaining 2 tablespoons of the vegetable oil over a medium-high heat in the other pan. Add the asafoetida and stir until it sizzles. Add the fenugreek seeds and stir until they turn darker. Add the onion with a pinch of salt and stir until it is softened, but not coloured.

Stir in the tomatoes, then add the coriander, chilli powder, cumin and turmeric. Season with salt and stir for 30 seconds to cook the spices. Watch closely so they do not burn. Add the yogurt, stirring all the ingredients together.

Reduce the heat to low and add all the sautéed mushrooms to the pan with the tomatoes and onion, stirring to combine all the ingredients. Adjust the seasoning with salt, if necessary, and stir in the chives just before serving, using a few extra chives for garnishing.

CALDIN MUSHROOM CURRY

Cogumelo Kari

This is a coconut milk-based Goan mushroom curry; flavourful and not too spicy. The earthiness of the mushrooms with tamarind and coconut are a real winner for me.

SERVES 4 AS A SHARING DISH

250g chestnut mushrooms
1 onion
fresh coriander leaves
2 tablespoons vegetable oil
1 tablespoon Onion Paste
   (page 218)
4 tablespoons Tamarind Liquid
   (page 223)
1 teaspoon ground turmeric
2 tablespoons frozen grated coconut,
   plus extra to garnish
125ml coconut milk
50ml water
sea salt

For the spice powder
1 or 2 large dried red chillies, to taste
2 tablespoons coriander seeds
1½ teaspoons cumin seeds

Assemble all the ingredients and equipment before you begin. You will need a spice grinder, a non-stick pan for toasting the spices and a large sauté or frying pan.

First, make the spice powder. Heat the dry non-stick pan over a high heat. Add the dried chillies and coriander and cumin seeds and stir until the spices are aromatic. Watch closely so the chillies don't burn before the spices toast. Transfer the chillies and seeds to the spice grinder and grind until a fine powder forms. Set aside.

Wipe, trim and quarter the mushrooms, including the caps and stalks. Halve, peel and thinly slice the onion. Rinse and chop enough coriander leaves to make about 2 tablespoons.

Heat the vegetable oil over a medium-high heat in the sauté pan. Add the onion with a pinch of salt and stir until it is softened, but not coloured. Add the mushrooms and continue stirring for 4–5 minutes until the mushrooms are tender and the onions are lightly coloured.

Add the onion paste and stir it into the onions and mushrooms for 30 seconds. Add the spice powder, tamarind liquid and turmeric, and continue stirring for 30 seconds to cook the spices. Stir in the frozen coconut, coconut milk and water, and set aside a little extra grated coconut to thaw. Season with salt and bring to the boil, stirring. Reduce the heat and leave to simmer for 2–3 minutes to blend the flavours. Stir in the chopped coriander just before serving and garnish with a little extra grated coconut.

GOAN SPINACH AND LENTILS

Goa Daal Palak

This is a very simple stir-fry recipe that can easily be doubled for a vegetarian main course. I think it goes particularly well with pilau, quinoa or chickpeas.

SERVES 4 AS A SHARING DISH

50g toor lentils (*toor daal*)
1 green chilli
1 small onion
1 tomato
2 tablespoons vegetable oil
1 teaspoon black mustard seeds
200g baby spinach leaves (see Atul's tip, page 105)
3 tablespoons frozen grated coconut, plus extra to garnish
sea salt

Bring a large covered saucepan of water to the boil and assemble all the ingredients and other equipment before you begin. You also need a sieve or colander and a wok or a large sauté or frying pan.

Rinse the lentils in the sieve with cold running water, then add them to the boiling water. Return the water to the boil and leave the lentils to boil, uncovered, for 20 minutes, or until they are tender, but still holding their shape.

Meanwhile, remove the stalk from the green chilli, if necessary, then slice the chilli lengthways. Peel, quarter and thinly slice the onion. Halve and slice the tomato.

Heat the vegetable oil over a medium-high heat in the wok. Add the mustard seeds and stir until they pop. Add the green chilli, onion and tomato with a pinch of salt, and continue stirring until the onion is softened, but not coloured. Turn the heat down and leave, uncovered and stirring occasionally, until the lentils have finished cooking.

Meanwhile, rinse the spinach and shake off the excess water.

Drain the lentils, then stir them into the sauté pan. Add the spinach and frozen coconut, season with salt and stir-fry until the spinach wilts. When you take the coconut out of the freezer set aside a little extra for the garnish.

Adjust the seasoning with salt, if necessary. Sprinkle with a little extra coconut just before serving – it will thaw in the residual heat.

SPICED GREEN BEANS AND LENTILS

Sem Ki Tarkari

Another way to cook this dish would be to blanch the green beans first and then stir them into the spices in the pan. This might be even a bit quicker, but my feeling is that you preserve more of the flavour by sautéing them instead. If you pour a small amount of vinaigrette dressing over any leftovers, you'll have an amazing salad.

SERVES 4 AS A SHARING DISH

90g split yellow mung dal
  (*moong daal*)
150g French (fine) beans
2cm piece of fresh ginger
1 long thin green chilli
2 tablespoons vegetable oil
1 teaspoon cumin seeds
1 teaspoon black mustard seeds
1 teaspoon split white lentils
  (*urid daal*)
1 large dried red chilli
10 fresh or dried curry leaves
2 teaspoons ground coriander
½ teaspoon red chilli powder, or
  to taste
6 tablespoons water
sea salt

Bring a covered saucepan of water to the boil and assemble all the ingredients and other equipment before you begin. You also need a sieve and a large sauté or frying pan with a lid.

Rinse the split yellow mung lentils in the sieve under cold running water, then add them to the boiling water. Return the water to the boil and boil the lentils, uncovered, for 15 minutes, or until tender. When they are tender, drain them well and set aside.

Meanwhile, top and tail the French beans, then cut them in half. Peel and chop the ginger – you want it finely chopped, but still to have some bite. Remove the stalk from the green chilli, if necessary, then finely chop the chilli.

Heat the vegetable oil over a medium-high heat in the sauté pan. Add the cumin and mustard seeds and stir until the cumin seeds crackle and the mustard seeds pop. Add the white lentils, lower the heat slightly, and continue stirring until they turn light brown. Watch closely so nothing burns. Add the dried chilli and stir it around to flavour the oil. Add the ginger, green chilli and the curry leaves, and stir for 30 seconds. Add the green beans and stir to incorporate all the spices. Add the ground coriander and chilli powder. Season with salt and stir for 30 seconds to cook the spices. Watch closely so they do not burn.

Stir in the water, cover the pan and leave the beans to cook for 7–8 minutes until they are tender-crisp.

When the beans are tender, add the yellow mung lentils and stir until combined and warmed through. Adjust the seasoning with salt, if necessary.

Atul's time-saving tip
Much to my mother's horror ('Atul, you waste so much'), the quickest way to top and tail the beans is to grab a handful and make sure the tips are all level with each other, then slice crossways. Turn the bunch around and repeat from the other end. It's certainly much quicker than trimming each bean individually.

TOMATO AND GARLIC DAL

Lasooni Daal

In Indian vegetarian families, lentil dishes are the main focus of the meal, replacing the meat. This is an easy recipe from the Punjab, with a pronounced garlic flavour.

I've added fresh coriander here for colour because of its year-round availability. When wild garlic is in season, however, finely chop the leaves and stir them into the tomato mixture at the end for an extra garlic hit, as well as for the colour. If you cook a knob of finely chopped ginger with the onions when using wild garlic the flavour is simply wonderful. Cooking onions is such a satisfying thing to do, and I've always loved the smell of onions being fried. Using rapeseed oil for this gives the dish a pungent flavour, but vegetable oil is equally good.

SERVES 4

4 garlic cloves
1 small thin green chilli
200g split yellow mung dal
   (*moong daal*)
2 teaspoons ground turmeric
several sprigs of fresh coriander
sea salt

For the tarka

4 garlic cloves
1 tomato
½ onion
2 tablespoons rapeseed or
   vegetable oil
1 teaspoon cumin seeds
2 teaspoons ground coriander
½ teaspoon red chilli powder, or
   to taste
½ teaspoon garam masala

Bring 750ml of water to the boil in a large covered saucepan and assemble all the ingredients and other equipment before you begin. You also need a sieve and a sauté or frying pan.

Peel and finely chop the garlic cloves. Remove the stalk from the green chilli, if necessary, and split the chilli lengthways, but leave it whole.

Rinse the lentils in the sieve with cold water, then add them to the boiling water and stir in the garlic, green chilli and turmeric. Return the water to the boil, then boil the lentils, uncovered, for 15 minutes, or until they are tender. When the lentils are tender, stir in extra water if they are too dry for you.

Meanwhile, to make the tarka, peel and finely chop the garlic cloves. Finely chop the tomato. Peel and finely chop the onion.

Heat the rapeseed oil over a medium-high heat in the pan. Add the garlic and cumin seeds and stir until the seeds crackle. Add the onion with a pinch of salt and continue to stir until the onion is lightly browned.

Add the ground coriander, chilli powder and garam masala, and stir for 30 seconds to cook the spices. Watch closely so they do not burn. Stir in the tomatoes, lower the heat and continue stirring until they soften and break down, pressing down with your spoon or spatula. Stir the tarka mixture into the lentils and bring to the boil.

Just before serving, rinse and finely chop the coriander sprigs. Stir half the chopped coriander into the lentils, then adjust the seasoning with salt, if necessary. Sprinkle over the remaining chopped coriander.

Atul's time-saving tip

Often when my wife, my mother-in-law or I intend to make this dish, we cook the lentils until they are just tender and then store them in a covered container in the fridge for up to four days. When we're ready to eat, all we have to do is quickly reheat the lentils, prepare the tarka and mix everything together, by which time the lentils will be perfectly tender.

TOMATOES AND LENTILS

Tamater Aur Mung Daal

The combination of seasonal tomatoes and mung dal is perfect in every way. Watch this recipe carefully and be sure to add the tomatoes towards the end of the cooking time as the acidity of the tomatoes could prevent the lentils from softening.

SERVES 4

1kg tomatoes
2 long thin green chillies
100g split yellow mung dal
  (*moong daal*)
1 tablespoon vegetable oil
2 tablespoons Onion Paste
  (page 218)
10 fresh or dried curry leaves
1 teaspoon red chilli powder, or
  to taste
½ teaspoon ground cumin
5 tablespoons water
sea salt

Bring a large covered saucepan of water to the boil and assemble all the ingredients and other equipment before you begin. You also need a sieve and a large sauté or frying pan with a lid.

Halve the tomatoes, then quarter each half. Remove the stalks from the green chillies, if necessary, and halve the chillies.

Rinse the lentils in the sieve with cold water, then add them to the boiling water. Return the water to the boil and leave the lentils to boil, uncovered, for 13 minutes, or until they are just tender. If the lentils were pasta, I'd say you want them al dente at this stage.

Meanwhile, heat the vegetable oil over a medium-high heat in the sauté pan. Add the onion paste and curry leaves and stir the paste into the oil for 30 seconds. Add the chilli powder and cumin and stir for a further 30 seconds to cook the spices. Watch closely so they do not burn.

Add the tomatoes, chillies and water to the pan, stirring to incorporate the onion paste and spices. Season with salt and bring to the boil, then turn the heat down to medium, cover the pan and leave the tomatoes to simmer and soften while the lentils finish cooking.

When the lentils are tender, drain them well. Stir the lentils into the tomatoes, increase the heat to medium and leave the mixture to bubble, uncovered, for about 2 minutes until the tomatoes are tender and the skins just start loosening, but they are still holding their shape, and the lentils are completely tender. You don't want the tomatoes to reduce to a sauce. Adjust the seasoning with salt, if necessary, and serve.

SOUR LENTILS

Khatti Daal

This is a straightforward supper dish, exactly what every Indian family cook makes regularly and the sort of recipe I cook when I'm at home with my family. My wife loves lentils, so she was the one who had to give the thumbs up to this recipe.

You'll notice I've used the dried red chilli to flavour the oil for the tarka, and then removed it from the pan after about twenty seconds. You can keep it in if you want, but it really does make the dish very, very hot, and that's not what I intended here. It's important not to add the tamarind liquid until the split mung dal are tender, because once the tamarind has been added they won't soften anymore.

SERVES 4

1 garlic clove
2cm piece of fresh ginger
fresh coriander leaves
200g split yellow mung dal
    (*moong daal*)
6 fresh or dried curry leaves
½ teaspoon red chilli powder, or
    to taste
½ teaspoon ground turmeric
sea salt

For the tarka

5 garlic cloves
2 long thin green chillies
2 tablespoons vegetable oil
1 large dried red chilli
1 teaspoon cumin seeds
10 fresh or dried curry leaves
6 tablespoons Tamarind Liquid (page
    223), or to taste

Bring 750ml of water to the boil in a large covered saucepan and assemble all the ingredients and other equipment before you begin. You will also need a sieve and a sauté or frying pan.

Peel and crush the garlic clove. Peel and thinly slice the ginger – remember this is a simple, rustic dish so you don't have to be too precise. Rinse and roughly chop enough coriander leaves to make about 3 tablespoons.

Rinse the lentils in the sieve with cold water, then add them to the boiling water. Stir in the garlic, sliced ginger, curry leaves, chilli powder and turmeric. Return the water to the boil, then leave the lentils to boil, uncovered, for 15 minutes, or until they are tender.

Meanwhile, prepare the ingredients for the tarka. Peel and thinly slice the garlic cloves. Remove the stalks from the green chillies, if necessary, and finely chop the chillies.

When the lentils are tender, make the tarka. Heat the vegetable oil over a high heat in the sauté pan. Add the dried red chilli and stir around for about 20 seconds to flavour the oil, then remove and set aside. Reduce the heat to medium-high, add the cumin seeds to the pan and stir until they crackle. Add the garlic, green chillies and curry leaves, and stir until the garlic is very lightly coloured. Watch closely so none of the ingredients burn.

Pull the pan off the heat and stir in the tamarind liquid. Tip the tarka into the lentils. Add the chopped coriander and stir together. Return the pan to the heat and boil for about 2 minutes to blend the flavours. Return the dried chilli to the pan, if you want an extra blast of heat. Adjust the seasoning with salt, if necessary, and serve.

Atul's time-saving tip

Although I've included a selection of pressure cooker recipes in this book, I know not everyone has one, so I've cooked this in a conventional manner. I do urge you, however, to invest in one of the modern pressure cookers if you want to cook lentils in a hurry. This dish would be on the table in less than fifteen minutes if cooked in a pressure cooker.

BENGALI LENTILS

Choler Daal

Every Indian household uses a pressure cooker, and, in my opinion, life without a pressure cooker in the kitchen is not good. Bengali food is cooked a lot in ghee, which I use here to fry fresh coconut and to add richness to the lentils. If you can't find fresh coconut chunks, however, don't fuss – just use the dried slices that you can buy in supermarkets and health-food shops.

SERVES 4

200g split yellow mung dal
   (*moong daal*)
1 long thin green chilli
2 teaspoons ground coriander
1 teaspoon red chilli powder, or
   to taste
1 teaspoon ground cumin
1 teaspoon garam masala
1 teaspoon ground turmeric
fresh coriander leaves
sea salt

For the fried coconut
50g fresh coconut pieces
1 tablespoon ghee

For the tarka
4 green cardamom pods
1 heaped tablespoon ghee
1 cinnamon stick
2 cloves
1 dried bay leaf

Assemble all the ingredients before you begin. You need a sieve, a pressure cooker (page 229), a non-stick sauté or frying pan, a plate lined with kitchen paper and a saucepan if your pressure cooker is a model that can't be placed on the hob.

Put the lentils in the sieve and rinse under cold water. I like to rinse them 2 or 3 times. Transfer them to the pressure cooker with enough water to cover them by 2.5cm. Stir in the chilli, ground coriander, chilli powder, ground cumin, garam masala and turmeric. Seal the lid and cook over a high heat to bring to high pressure. Reduce the heat to maintain pressure and cook for 10 minutes, or according to the manufacturer's instructions.

Meanwhile, slice the fresh coconut very thinly to use as a garnish. Melt 1 tablespoon of ghee over a medium-high heat in the non-stick pan. Add the coconut pieces and fry, constantly moving the pieces around, for about 2 minutes until browned and crisp. Watch closely so they do not burn, which can happen very quickly. Transfer to the paper-lined plate and set aside. Wipe out the pan and set aside.

Rinse and chop enough coriander leaves to make about 2 tablespoons.

When the lentils are cooked, release the pressure according to the manufacturer's instructions, then remove the lid. Season with salt. Place the pressure cooker over a high heat and leave any excess liquid to evaporate while you prepare the tarka. (If your pressure cooker can't be used on the hob, transfer the lentils to a saucepan.)

To make the tarka, lightly crush the cardamom pods to release the seeds. Melt 1 heaped tablespoon of ghee over a medium-high heat in the non-stick pan. Add the cinnamon stick and stir to flavour the oil. Add the cardamom pods and the seeds, cloves and bay leaf, and stir until the pods crackle.

Tip the ghee and spices into the lentils and stir together. Adjust the seasoning with salt, if necessary, and stir in the chopped coriander. Garnish with the coconut strips to serve.

GUJERATI LENTILS

Trevti Daal

Normally I would soak the lentils before cooking, but by using a pressure cooker in this recipe, it isn't necessary.

SERVES 4

200g toor lentils (*toor daal*)
2 tablespoons split yellow mung dal (*moong daal*)
1 tablespoon gram dal (*channa daal*)
1 teaspoon ground turmeric
sea salt

For the tarka

2 tomatoes
3 tablespoons vegetable oil
½ teaspoon asafoetida
2 cloves
5cm piece of cinnamon stick
1 teaspoon black mustard seeds
1 teaspoon red chilli powder, or to taste

Assemble all the ingredients and equipment before you begin. You need a sieve, a pressure cooker (page 229), a non-stick pan for cooking the tarka and a saucepan if your pressure cooker is a model that can't be placed on the hob.

Put the three types of pulses in the sieve and rinse under cold water. I like to rinse them 2 or 3 times. Transfer them to the pressure cooker with enough water to cover them by 2.5cm. Stir in the turmeric.

Seal the lid and cook over a high heat to bring to high pressure. Reduce the heat to maintain pressure and cook for 10 minutes, or according to the manufacturer's instructions.

Meanwhile, make the tarka. Finely chop the tomatoes. Heat the vegetable oil over a medium-high heat in the non-stick pan. Add the asafoetida and stir until it sizzles. Add the cloves, cinnamon stick and mustard seeds, and stir until the mustard seeds pop. Add the tomatoes and chilli powder and keep stirring for 30 seconds to cook the chilli powder and for the tomatoes to start softening. Turn the heat down and leave the tomatoes to cook very slowly, uncovered and stirring occasionally, until softened.

When the lentils are cooked, release the pressure according to the manufacturer's instructions, then remove the lid. Season with salt. Place the pressure cooker over a high heat, pour in the tarka and bring to the boil, stirring. (If your pressure cooker can't be used on the hob, transfer the lentils to a saucepan.) Adjust the seasoning with salt, if necessary, and serve.

CHICKPEA AND KALE CURRY

Kabuli Chana Aur Kale

Chickpea and spinach curry is quite a common dish in India, but as I had some kale handy I decided to devise this version – and I have to say, I'm very pleased with the result. I hope you will be, too.

You can replace the water with vegetable or chicken stock, if you want, but it's really not necessary. This is a quick-and-easy curry, and one of those dishes I would just put in the middle of the table for everyone to help themselves.

SERVES 4 AS A SHARING DISH

1 x 400g can chickpeas
2 garlic cloves
1 long thin green chilli
½ onion
2.5cm piece of fresh ginger
1½ tablespoons vegetable oil
1 teaspoon cumin seeds
2 teaspoons ground coriander
1 teaspoon ground cumin
½ teaspoon red chilli powder
½ teaspoon ground turmeric
300ml water
100g shredded kale leaves
125ml coconut milk
½ lemon (optional)
sea salt

Assemble all the ingredients and equipment before you begin. You need a sieve and a wok or a large sauté or frying pan.

Drain and rinse the chickpeas in the sieve with cold water, then set aside. Peel and thinly slice the garlic cloves. Remove the stalk from the green chilli, if necessary, then finely chop the chilli. Peel and thinly slice the onion. Peel and finely chop the ginger.

Heat the vegetable oil over a medium-high heat in the wok. Add the cumin seeds and stir until they crackle. Add the garlic and green chilli and stir for 30 seconds to flavour the oil. Add the onion with a pinch of salt and continue stirring until it is softened, but not coloured. Add the ginger and stir for a further 30 seconds.

Add the chickpeas to the pan and stir to coat them in the oil and spices. Add the ground coriander, ground cumin, chilli powder and turmeric, and stir for 30 seconds to cook the spices. Watch closely so they do not burn. Stir in 125ml of the water to prevent the spices from catching on the bottom of the pan, gently crushing about one-tenth of the chickpeas as you stir to thicken the gravy slightly.

Add the kale to the pan with the remaining 175ml water. Season with salt, turn the heat up to high and stir until the kale wilts. Stir in the coconut milk and leave the curry to bubble, uncovered, for 8 minutes, or until the kale is tender and the liquid reduces by about three-quarters.

Adjust the flavours with lemon juice and salt, if necessary, and then serve.

Atul's time-saving tip

In my restaurants, I would use whole kale leaves and finely chop the stalks, but in the interest of speed here, I suggest you buy a bag of shredded kale leaves. If you have the whole leaves and aren't in a hurry, however, be sure to include the stalks for extra texture and flavour.

CHICKPEA AND POTATO CURRY

Ghugni

This recipe is very near to my heart. There is a lovely restaurant in Kolkata called Kewpie's Kitchen. It's in a family's living room and whenever I'm in Kolkata, I try to eat there. It's one of my favourite restaurants in the world. It's very nostalgic to think about, because I've been going there since I was a child, when I went with my dad, and this is one of the dishes we always ordered.

I absolutely hate waste in the kitchen, so use the ghee you cook the potatoes in to make the tarka with. If you don't have a piece of fresh coconut, that's not a reason not to make this particular recipe. Just omit the coconut.

SERVES 4 AS A SHARING DISH

10 well-scrubbed new potatoes (see Atul's tip, page 29)
4 tablespoons ghee or vegetable oil
50g fresh coconut pieces (optional)
1 x 400g can chickpeas
1 dried bay leaf
1 tablespoon Onion Paste (page 218)
1 teaspoon ground turmeric
500ml water
3cm piece of fresh ginger
fresh coriander leaves
sea salt

For the spice powder

6 cloves
4 green cardamom pods
1 cinnamon stick
2 teaspoons coriander seeds
1 teaspoon cumin seeds
1 teaspoon black peppercorns

For the tarka

1½ teaspoons ghee reserved from cooking the potatoes
1 large dried red chilli
1 teaspoon fennel seeds

Assemble all the ingredients before you begin. You need 2 large sauté or frying pans (one of which is non-stick), a sieve, a non-stick pan for toasting the spices and a spice grinder.

Get the potatoes cooking as soon as possible. Chop the potatoes into 1cm dice. Melt 3 tablespoons of the ghee over a high heat in the non-stick sauté pan. Add the potatoes and fry, stirring occasionally, for about 8 minutes until almost tender and golden brown.

Meanwhile, slice the fresh coconut very thinly, if using. Drain and rinse the chickpeas in the sieve, then set the sieve aside.

Next, make the spice powder. Heat the dry non-stick pan over a high heat. Add the cloves, cardamom pods, cinnamon stick, coriander and cumin seeds and peppercorns, and stir until they are aromatic. Transfer the spices to the spice grinder and grind until a fine powder forms. Set aside. Wipe out the pan and set aside.

Melt the remaining 1 tablespoon of ghee over a medium-high heat in the other sauté pan. Add the coconut and fry, constantly moving the pieces around, for about 2 minutes until the slices are browned and crisp. Watch closely so they do not burn. Transfer to kitchen paper and set aside.

Add the chickpeas, bay leaf and onion paste to the ghee remaining in the pan, and stir for 30 seconds. Add the spice powder and turmeric. Season with salt and stir for a further 30 seconds to cook the turmeric and coat the chickpeas in spices. Watch closely so the spices do not burn. Strain the potatoes in the sieve, reserving the excess ghee. Tip the potatoes into the pan with the chickpeas, add the water and bring to the boil, stirring. Leave to boil, uncovered, for about 5 minutes until the potatoes are completely tender and the gravy has reduced.

While the potatoes finish cooking, peel and finely chop the ginger. Rinse and chop enough coriander leaves to make about 2 tablespoons.

Just before serving, make the tarka. Heat the reserved ghee over a high heat in the non-stick pan that you used to toast the spices in. Add the dried chilli and fennel seeds and stir until the seeds crackle. Tip into the potatoes and chickpeas and stir together. Adjust the seasoning with salt, if necessary, and stir in the chopped ginger and the chopped coriander. Sprinkle over the coconut slices to garnish, if using.

PANEER AND BLACK CHICKPEA CURRY

Paneer Chana Curry

The combination of fresh ginger and black chickpeas always works incredibly well. I can remember my mother making this Punjabi recipe and she always stirred in about two tablespoons of yogurt at the end to bring everything together, but I prefer this lighter version. I've specified using mild green chillies, so there isn't any need to de-seed them. If you aren't sure how hot your chilli is, however, taste the tip; even a tiny piece will give you an idea as to how hot it is.

SERVES 4

500g paneer
2 x 400g cans black chickpeas, or ordinary canned chickpeas
4 black cardamom pods
6 tablespoons vegetable oil
6 cloves
¼ teaspoon black peppercorns
2 bay leaves
1 cinnamon stick
2 teaspoons cumin seeds
4 teaspoons ground coriander
½ teaspoon red chilli powder, or to taste
½ teaspoon ground dried fenugreek leaf powder
½ teaspoon ground turmeric
½ teaspoon mango powder (*amchur*), or lemon juice
2 tomatoes
2 thick green chillies
5cm piece of fresh ginger
fresh coriander leaves
¼ teaspoon garam masala
sea salt

Assemble all the ingredients and equipment before you begin. You need a bowl of hot water large enough to hold the cubed paneer, a colander or sieve and a large sauté or frying pan.

Cut the paneer into bite-sized cubes, then put it in a bowl of hot water to soften before cooking. Drain and rinse the chickpeas well. Lightly crush the black cardamom pods to loosen the seeds.

Heat the vegetable oil over a medium-high heat in the pan. Add the cardamom pods with the seeds, the cloves, peppercorns, bay leaves and cinnamon stick, and stir for 30 seconds. You want to flavour the oil really well at this point. Add the cumin seeds and continue stirring until they crackle.

Add the chickpeas to the pan, season with salt and stir to mix together. Stir in the ground coriander, chilli powder, ground fenugreek, turmeric and mango powder, and continue stirring for 30 seconds to cook the spices. (If you are substituting lemon juice for the mango powder, add it later with the garam masala.) Watch closely so the spices do not burn.

Drain the paneer and add it to the pan. Season with salt, turn the heat to low and leave to cook, stirring occasionally, while you prepare the remaining ingredients.

Coarsely chop the tomatoes. Remove the stalks from the green chillies, if necessary, then finely chop the chillies. Peel and very finely chop the ginger. Chop enough coriander leaves to make 4 tablespoons.

Stir the tomatoes, green chilli and three-quarters of each of the chopped ginger and chopped coriander into the pan. Increase the heat to medium and stir, gently crushing the tomatoes with the back of your spoon, for about 5 minutes.

Stir in the garam masala. Increase the heat to medium-high and continue stirring until the tomatoes are softened, but not completely crushed. Adjust the seasoning with salt, if necessary, and sprinkle with the remaining chopped coriander and ginger to serve.

SPICED RED KIDNEY BEANS

Rajma

Some pulses cook within thirty minutes, but you really have to use the canned variety of kidney beans for quick cooking. Even though the beans are cooked, they can still be a bit tough if they have been in the can for a long time, so I add lots of water during the cooking process to soften them more.

SERVES 4

2 x 400g cans red kidney beans
800g Greek-style yogurt
60g ghee, or 4 tablespoons
    vegetable oil
¼ teaspoon ground asafoetida
2 teaspoons cumin seeds
2 tablespoons ground coriander
2 teaspoons ground ginger
1 teaspoon red chilli powder, or
    to taste
660ml water
160ml passata
10cm piece of fresh ginger
fresh coriander leaves
3 teaspoons garam masala
½ lemon
sea salt

Assemble all the ingredients and equipment before you begin. You need a sieve, a whisk, a bowl and a large sauté or frying pan.

Drain and rinse the kidney beans in the sieve with cold water. Whisk the yogurt in the bowl, then set aside.

Melt the ghee over a medium-high heat in the pan. Add the asafoetida and stir until it sizzles. Add the cumin seeds and stir until they crackle. Add all but 6 tablespoons of the yogurt and continue stirring for 2–3 minutes. It's very important to cook the yogurt well at this stage. Stir in the ground coriander, ground ginger and chilli powder. Season with salt and continue stirring for a further minute to cook the spices. Watch closely so nothing burns.

Stir in about 80ml of the water and all the passata and bring to the boil. Add the kidney beans and leave the gravy to gently boil, uncovered and stirring occasionally, while you prepare the remaining ingredients.

Meanwhile, peel and very finely chop the fresh ginger. Rinse and chop enough coriander leaves to make about 3 tablespoons.

When the liquid has evaporated, stir in the remaining 580ml water and return the gravy to the boil. Stir in 2 tablespoons of the chopped ginger and continue gently boiling for about 1 minute until the fat comes to the surface.

Stir in 1 teaspoon of the garam masala and continue gently boiling for a further 5 minutes, stirring occasionally, until the gravy thickens. Squeeze in about 1 teaspoon of lemon juice and continue boiling for 30 seconds.

Reduce the heat to low, then stir in the remaining yogurt, the remaining 2 teaspoons of garam masala, the remaining chopped ginger and 2 tablespoons of the chopped coriander. Leave to simmer for 30 seconds for the flavours to blend. Adjust the seasoning with salt, if necessary, then sprinkle with the remaining chopped coriander before serving.

PEA AND PEANUT CURRY

Shingdane ani Vatanis Chi Bhaji

This is such a simple dish from the Mumbai region, where peanuts often feature in recipes. It has beautiful flavours.

SERVES 4 AS A SHARING DISH

230g blanched unsalted raw peanuts
2 tablespoons ghee
2½ teaspoons cumin seeds
1 large dried red chilli
¼ teaspoon caster sugar
250ml water
250g frozen peas
175ml coconut milk
fresh coriander leaves
sea salt

For the paste
1 long thin green chilli
3cm piece of cinnamon stick
4 cloves
5 tablespoons frozen grated coconut
2 tablespoons water

Assemble all the ingredients and equipment before you begin. You will need a spice grinder, a food processor fitted with a chopping blade and a large sauté or frying pan.

First put 30g of the peanuts in the spice grinder and grind until a fine powder forms, which will be used to thicken the curry. Set aside.

To make the paste, remove the stalk from the green chilli, if necessary, then coarsely chop the chilli. Put the cinnamon stick and cloves in the spice grinder and grind until a fine powder forms. Transfer the powder to a food processor, add the green chilli, frozen coconut and water, and blitz, scraping down the sides of the bowl, if necessary, until a coarse paste forms. Set aside.

Melt the ghee over a medium-high heat in the pan. Add the cumin seeds and dried red chilli and fry until the seeds crackle. Stir in the remaining 200g of peanuts, the sugar and a pinch of salt, and continue stirring for about 2 minutes until the peanuts are lightly coloured. Turn the heat down to low and stir in the paste. The aroma at this point should be absolutely beautiful.

Continue stirring until the liquid evaporates and the paste is fried, then stir in the water. Watch closely so the paste doesn't burn. Add the ground peanut powder, increase the heat and continue simmering, stirring occasionally, for 2 minutes. Add the peas and coconut milk and bring to the boil, stirring. Reduce the heat slightly and leave the curry to simmer.

Meanwhile, rinse and finely chop enough coriander leaves to make about 2 tablespoons.

Stir half the chopped coriander into the curry. Continue simmering for a further 2–3 minutes until the peas are cooked and tender.

Adjust the seasoning with salt, if necessary, then sprinkle with the remaining chopped coriander just before serving.

Atul's time-saving tip
Frozen peas are such a great freezer stand-by, especially when you are cooking in a hurry. When fresh peas are available, however, and if you have time to shell them, you need about 500g peas in the pod.

EGGS AND CHEESE

BENGALI EGG AND POTATO CURRY

Dimer Aloo Jhol

This is a straightforward, everyday family dish, with starch and protein in one bowl. These eggs are soft-boiled, but if you prefer firmer yolks simmer them for an extra three minutes.

SERVES 4

4 eggs
8 well-scrubbed new potatoes (see Atul's tips, below)
4 green cardamom pods
1 small onion
2 tablespoons vegetable oil
2 dried bay leaves
1 cinnamon stick
2 cloves
2 tablespoons Onion Paste (page 218)
1 teaspoon ground turmeric
½ teaspoon red chilli powder, or to taste
600ml water
4 tablespoons passata
fresh coriander leaves
¼ teaspoon garam masala
sea salt

Bring a large covered saucepan of water to the boil and assemble all the ingredients and other equipment before you begin. You also need a large sauté or frying pan, a colander or sieve and a bowl large enough to hold the shelled eggs.

Carefully lower the eggs into the pan of boiling water and add a large pinch of salt. Be careful the water doesn't splash you as you add them. Cover the pan and return the water to the boil, then turn the heat to a low boil so the bubbles just break the surface and boil the eggs, uncovered, for 5 minutes for soft-boiled.

Meanwhile, cut the potatoes into 0.5cm slices. Lightly crush the cardamom pods to loosen the seeds. Peel, halve and thinly slice the onion.

When the eggs have finished cooking, drain and run them under cold water to stop the cooking and make them cool enough to handle. Return them to the pan and set aside.

Heat the vegetable oil over a medium-high heat in the sauté pan. Add the bay leaves and cinnamon stick and stir around to flavour the oil. Add the cardamom pods and the seeds and the cloves and stir until the spices crackle. Add the onion with a pinch of salt and stir occasionally until softened, but not coloured.

Add the onion paste and stir for 30 seconds. Stir in the potato slices and season with salt. Add the turmeric and chilli powder and stir for 30 seconds to cook the spices. Watch closely so they do not burn.

Add the water and passata and bring to the boil, stirring, then leave the gravy to bubble for 10–12 minutes until the potato slices are tender.

While the gravy is simmering, shell the eggs and set them aside in the bowl until the potatoes are tender. Rinse and chop enough coriander leaves to make about 2 tablespoons, reserving some whole leaves for garnishing.

When the potatoes are tender, add the whole eggs, garam masala and the chopped coriander. Leave to simmer for a minute or so, just to blend the flavours. Adjust the seasoning with salt, if necessary, then sprinkle with whole coriander leaves just before serving.

Atul's time-saving tips

You might be surprised to see that I add salt to the water when boiling eggs, but it makes the shells easier and, therefore, quicker to peel. I also buy scrubbed, ready-to-cook new potatoes so I don't have to spend time cleaning them.

TOMATOES AND EGGS

Tamater Pe Eeda

Here is another recipe inspired by India's Parsee community, known for their many combinations of vegetables cooked with eggs. It is most unusual, however, to find cucumber in Indian cooking, but the Parsees are ingenious at making use of everything, quite rightly. In any recipe, when the fresh tomatoes break down – just before the eggs are added in this recipe – I think is the point when a dish comes alive.

This flavoursome, straightforward supper dish can also be made with courgettes, but I love cucumber and think it has such a lovely effect on your body. The canned chopped tomatoes are included to add body and help harmonise the flavours.

SERVES 4

4 juicy tomatoes
1 long thin green chilli
½ cucumber, about 250g
½ lemon
fresh coriander leaves
1½ teaspoons vegetable oil
½ teaspoon red chilli powder, or
   to taste
½ teaspoon caster sugar
½ teaspoon turmeric
¼ teaspoon ground cinnamon
½ teaspoon ground cumin
3 tablespoons Onion Paste
   (page 218)
4 tablespoons canned
   chopped tomatoes
4 eggs
sea salt and freshly ground
   black pepper

Assemble all the ingredients before you begin. You need a large sauté or frying pan with a lid.

Coarsely chop the tomatoes. Remove the stalk from the green chilli, if necessary, then finely chop the chilli. Quarter the piece of cucumber lengthways, then de-seed and cut into 0.5cm dice. Squeeze 1 tablespoon of lemon juice. Rinse and chop enough coriander leaves to make about 1 tablespoon.

Heat the vegetable oil over a medium-high heat in the pan. Add the chilli powder, sugar, turmeric, ground cinnamon and ground cumin, and stir for 30 seconds to cook the spices. Watch closely so they do not burn. Add the onion paste and continue stirring for a further 30 seconds.

Lower the heat to medium. Add the chopped fresh tomatoes and lemon juice. Season with salt and stir for a couple of minutes until the tomatoes just start breaking down. Stir in the canned tomatoes and the green chilli. Cover the pan and leave the mixture to simmer for about 2 minutes.

Stir in the cucumber and season with freshly ground pepper. Re-cover the pan and leave the mixture to simmer for a further 2 minutes, or until the fresh tomatoes are almost broken down. Adjust the seasoning with salt, if necessary.

Use the back of your spoon or spatula to smooth the surface of the tomato mixture. One by one, crack the eggs into a small bowl, then gently tip them into the tomato mixture. Cover the pan and leave the mixture over a medium heat for 6 minutes, or until the whites are set, but the yolks are still runny. Sprinkle with the coriander before serving.

PUNJABI EGG CURRY

Punjabi Anda Curry

This is a great recipe, especially when it comes to feeding a family quickly. It works incredibly well as it is, but it's very adaptable. Cumin seeds, chilli and ginger are the defining flavour of most egg curries like this one, and no matter what else you add these flavours take centre stage. If my mother was making an egg curry when I was growing up during rationing, for example, she would include some diced boiled potatoes, as I have done for the photo here – and it's a great way to use leftover potatoes. (Or, she might just use the potatoes with this gravy, in which case it becomes *Punjabi aloo curry*.) Another option is to fry the whole boiled egg in the spices just to get a nice spicy coat, especially popular in East India, where I grew up (see Andhra Egg Curry, page 102).

Growing up in India, everybody ate hard-boiled eggs. Nobody liked soft-boiled eggs, unfortunately, but after living in Britain for so long I am now a fan of soft-boiled eggs. They look beautiful, in my opinion, and they taste better. If you prefer a firmer yolk, however, cook the eggs for a minute longer.

SERVES 4

6 eggs
2cm piece of fresh ginger
1 thin long green chilli
½ onion
2 tablespoons vegetable oil
1 teaspoon cumin seeds
2 tomatoes
1 teaspoon ground coriander
¼ teaspoon red chilli powder, or
    to taste
¼ teaspoon ground turmeric
2 tablespoons Onion Masala
    (page 222)
250ml water
fresh coriander leaves
¼ teaspoon dried fenugreek
    leaf powder
¼ teaspoon garam masala
sea salt

Bring a large covered saucepan of water to the boil and assemble all the ingredients and other equipment before you begin. You also need a large sauté or frying pan with a lid and a bowl large enough to hold the shelled eggs.

Carefully lower the eggs into the boiling water and add a large pinch of salt. Be careful the water doesn't splash you as you add them. Cover the pan and return the water to the boil, then turn the heat to a low boil so bubbles just break the surface and boil the eggs, uncovered, for 5 minutes for soft-boiled.

Drain the eggs and rinse under cold running water to stop the cooking. Return them to the pan and cover with cold water, then set aside until required.

Meanwhile, peel and finely chop the ginger. Remove the stalk end from the green chilli, if necessary, then finely chop the chilli. Peel and thinly slice the onion.

Heat the vegetable oil over a medium-high heat in the sauté pan. Add the ginger, chilli and cumin seeds, and stir until the seeds crackle. Add the onion with a pinch of salt and stir occasionally until it is lightly coloured.

While the onions are frying, coarsely chop the tomatoes.

Add the ground coriander, chilli powder and turmeric to the onion, and stir for 30 seconds to cook the spices. Add the onion masala and stir for a further 30 seconds. Add 125ml of the water and stir for 30 seconds. Add the tomatoes and leave them to begin softening while you shell the eggs. Put the eggs in the bowl as they are shelled, then set aside.

Stir the remaining 125ml of the water into the pan and adjust the seasoning with salt. Cover the pan and leave to simmer for about 5 minutes for the flavours to blend and the tomatoes to soften, but not disintegrate.

Rinse and chop enough coriander leaves to make about 1 tablespoon.

Stir the dried fenugreek powder and garam masala into the gravy, then adjust the seasoning with salt, if necessary. Halve the soft-boiled eggs and gently stir them into the gravy. Transfer the curry to a serving bowl and sprinkle with the chopped coriander.

STIR-FRIED OKRA AND EGGS

Kacang Bendi

When you can't find fresh okra, frozen works just as well, and various brands are sold already chopped. Add it straight from the freezer and it should cook in about the same time. Just make sure it is perfectly tender before adding the eggs. If you want to make a larger portion, all the ingredients can be doubled.

SERVES 2 AS A SHARING DISH

200g okra
3 garlic cloves
2 thick long fresh red chillies
1 large dried red chilli
1 banana shallot, or 2 ordinary shallots
2 eggs
3 tablespoons vegetable oil
1½ tablespoons Tamarind Liquid (page 223)
light soy sauce, to taste
sea salt

Assemble all the ingredients and equipment before you begin. You need a bowl and a large wok or a large sauté or frying pan.

Rinse and trim the stalk ends from the okra pods, then thinly slice the pods on the diagonal. Peel and thinly slice the garlic cloves. Remove the stalks from the fresh red chillies, if necessary, then thinly slice the chillies on the diagonal. Remove the stalk from the dried red chilli, if necessary, then slice the chilli. Peel and finely chop the shallot.

Beat the eggs together in the bowl and season with salt. Set aside.

Heat the wok over a high heat. When it is hot, add the vegetable oil and swirl it around. Lower the heat to medium-high, add the dried chilli and stir to flavour the oil. Add the garlic, fresh red chillies and shallots, and stir-fry until the shallots are softened, but not coloured.

Add the okra and continue stir-frying for 5 minutes, or until the okra is tender. Stir in the tamarind liquid and soy sauce to taste.

Push the okra around the side of the pan, then pour the eggs into the 'hole' in the centre and scramble. When the eggs start to set, stir in the okra until everything is mixed. Adjust the seasoning with soy sauce, if necessary.

Atul's time-saving tip
Cutting the okra on the diagonal helps them cook quicker.

ANDHRA EGG CURRY

Bhagar-e-Anda

From Hyderabad, where food is still greatly influenced by the legacy of the Muslim Mogul rulers, this straightforward recipe also showcases the influence of southern Indian cuisine with the coconut and tamarind liquid.

SERVES 4

8 eggs
2 garlic cloves
1 long thin green chilli
vegetable oil
¼ teaspoon fenugreek seeds
10 fresh or dried curry leaves
1 dried red chilli
½ teaspoon cumin seeds
3 teaspoons ground coriander
2 teaspoons ground cumin
1½ teaspoons red chilli powder, or
    to taste
2 teaspoons ground turmeric
2 tablespoons Tamarind Liquid
    (page 223)
250ml water
125ml coconut milk
1 teaspoon garam masala
sea salt

For the spice powder

1½ tablespoons white
    sesame seeds
1 tablespoon desiccated coconut
1 tablespoon frozen grated coconut
1½ teaspoons white poppy seeds

Bring a large covered saucepan of water to the boil and assemble all the ingredients and other equipment before you begin. You also need a non-stick pan for toasting the spices, a spice grinder, a large non-stick sauté or frying pan and a bowl large enough to hold the hard-boiled eggs.

Carefully lower the eggs into the boiling water with a large pinch of salt. Be careful the water doesn't splash you as you add them. Cover the pan and return the water to the boil, then boil the eggs, uncovered, for 8 minutes to hard-boil.

Meanwhile, make the spice powder. Heat the dry non-stick pan over a low heat. Add the sesame seeds, desiccated and frozen coconut and poppy seeds and stir until everything is lightly toasted and aromatic. Watch closely so nothing burns. Tip the mixture into the spice grinder and grind until a fine powder forms. Set aside. Wipe out the pan and set aside.

When the eggs have finished cooking, drain them and run them under cold water to stop the cooking and make them cool enough to handle. Set aside. Peel and thinly slice the garlic cloves. Remove the stalk from the green chilli, if necessary, then finely chop the chilli.

Heat 2 tablespoons of vegetable oil over a medium-high heat in the sauté pan. Add the fenugreek seeds and stir until they turn darker. Add curry leaves, dried chilli and cumin seeds, and stir until the cumin seeds crackle. Add the spice powder, garlic and green chilli, and stir for 30 seconds. Add 2 teaspoons of the ground coriander, 1 teaspoon of the ground cumin, ½ teaspoon of the chilli powder and ½ teaspoon of the turmeric, and stir for a further 30 seconds to cook the spices. Watch closely so the spices do not burn.

Stir in the tamarind liquid, water and coconut milk. Season with salt and continue stirring to blend the flavours. Leave the curry to simmer, uncovered, while you shell and fry the eggs.

Shell the eggs, pat them dry with kitchen paper and transfer to the bowl. Add about 1 teaspoon vegetable oil to the eggs, then add the remaining 1 teaspoon ground coriander, 1 teaspoon ground cumin, 1 teaspoon chilli powder, 1½ teaspoons ground turmeric and the garam masala. Season with salt and stir together so the eggs are smeared with the spices.

Heat a very thin layer of vegetable oil over a high heat in the non-stick pan you used to toast the spices. Add the eggs and fry, stirring, for 1 minute, or until the spices are golden brown.

Fry the eggs in batches, if necessary, and watch closely so the spices do not burn.

Reduce the heat under the gravy and gently stir in the eggs. Adjust the seasoning with salt, if necessary, then transfer the curry to a serving dish.

KALE AND SPINACH WITH EGGS

Bhajui Pe Voda

Eggs and spinach – such a universal combination, and this dish is inspired by the large Parsee community where I grew up. Some people like to pan-fry the onions until they are absolutely brown, but I like to keep them translucent, so you can retain the texture and the flavour of the onion. Onions really have a lot to say, in my opinion. This dish is great served with naans.

SERVES 4

2 tomatoes
2 onions
2 tablespoons vegetable oil
3 garlic cloves
1 long thin green chilli
5cm piece of fresh ginger
125ml water (optional)
200g shredded kale leaves (see Atul's tip, below)
200g baby spinach leaves (see Atul's tip, below)
small handful of fresh coriander leaves
1½ teaspoons ground coriander
1 teaspoon red chilli powder, or to taste
1 teaspoon ground cumin
4 eggs
sea salt

Assemble all the ingredients and equipment before you begin. You need a large sauté or frying pan with a lid, a food processor fitted with a chopping blade and a colander or sieve.

Coarsely chop the tomatoes. Peel, halve and thinly slice the onions. Heat the vegetable oil over a medium-high heat in the pan. Add the onions with a pinch of salt and leave them to soften, stirring occasionally, while you make a paste. You want them soft, but not coloured.

Meanwhile, peel the garlic cloves. Remove the stalk from the green chilli, if necessary, then coarsely chop the chilli. Peel and coarsely chop the ginger. Put the garlic cloves, green chilli and ginger in the food processor, and blitz until a fine green paste forms. Add the paste to the onions and stir until blended and the onions are softened. Stir in the water, if necessary, to prevent the onions catching on the bottom of the pan and burning.

Rinse the kale leaves, spinach leaves and fresh coriander. Tear out any thick stalks from the kale, if necessary, and drop the leaves into the pan along with the spinach leaves. Tear the coriander leaves from the stalks and add the leaves to the pan; discard the stalks.

Add the ground coriander, chilli powder and ground cumin to the pan. Season with salt and stir the leaves and spices together for 30 seconds to cook the spices. The leaves will start wilting and shrinking in volume. Add the tomatoes and continue stirring until all the ingredients are blended. Adjust the seasoning with salt, if necessary.

Spread out the spinach mixture over the bottom of the pan, then use your spoon or spatula to make 4 indentations. One by one, crack the eggs into a small bowl, then gently tip them into the indentations. Cover the pan and leave the mixture over a medium heat for 6 minutes, or until the whites are set but the yolks are still runny and then serve.

Atul's time-saving tip
Buying a bag of shredded kale and using baby spinach leaves helps save you prep time. If you do buy whole kale leaves or large spinach leaves, however, rinse them thoroughly, then cut out the thick stalks and finely shred the leaves.

SEAFOOD

MARATHI CLAMS

Marathi Tisrya

I have cooked with a Marathi chef in my kitchen for a long time. He sent me a recipe for a clam dish, but, frankly, it was a bit complicated for me, so I have re-created the recipe for my purpose – and for your purpose, too, I hope.

When you can't get live clams, substitute live mussels. Clean them like the clams, but also scrape off any barnacles when rinsing and pull away the 'beards' that are attached. Cook for three to four minutes until they are all open, and discard any that aren't open.

SERVES 2

1kg live clams
2 garlic cloves
3 tablespoons vegetable oil
1 teaspoon cumin seeds
1 teaspoon red chilli powder
1 teaspoon garam masala
2 tablespoons Onion Paste
  (page 218)
50g desiccated coconut
4 tablespoons canned chopped
  tomatoes
375ml water
½ lemon
fresh coriander leaves
salt

Assemble all the ingredients and equipment before you begin. You will need a colander and 2 large sauté or frying pans, one of which has a lid.

Put the clams in the colander and rinse well with cold water, scrubbing each with a stiff brush. Discard any with broken shells and any open ones that do not snap shut when you tap them sharply. Shake the excess water off the clams, dry with a kitchen towel and set them aside. Peel and finely chop the garlic cloves.

Heat 2 tablespoons of the vegetable oil over a medium-high heat in the pan without a lid. Add the cumin seeds and fry until they crackle. Add the chilli powder and garam masala and stir for 30 seconds. Add the onion paste and stir it into the oil for 30 seconds. Watch closely so nothing burns.

Lower the heat, add the coconut and continue stirring until it starts to lightly brown. Stir in the canned tomatoes. Season with salt, turn the heat to medium and stir for a further 30 seconds. Add 250ml of the water, stirring to blend all the ingredients. Leave to simmer, stirring occasionally, while you cook the clams.

Meanwhile, heat the remaining 1 tablespoon of the vegetable oil over a medium-high heat in the pan with a lid. Add the garlic and stir to flavour the oil. Add the clams and stir them around, then add the remaining 125ml water, cover the pan, turn the heat to high and leave the clams to cook for 1½ minutes, shaking the pan occasionally, or until all the clams open. Discard any that remain closed.

While the clams are cooking, squeeze 2 teaspoons of lemon juice and chop enough coriander leaves to make about 2 tablespoons.

Stir the clams with their cooking juices into the pan with the tomato mixture, then stir in the lemon juice and the chopped coriander. Adjust the seasoning of the gravy with salt, if necessary, and then serve.

ANDHRA PRAWN CURRY

Veinchana Royyalu

Andhraiites typically eat fiery hot food, but this prawn curry packs a lot of flavours too!

SERVES 4

500g raw peeled tiger prawns
6 green cardamom pods
fresh coriander sprigs
2 tablespoons vegetable oil
4 cloves
1 teaspoon fennel seeds
4 tablespoons Onion Paste
　　(page 218)
4 teaspoons ground coriander
1 teaspoon red chilli powder, or
　　to taste
125ml passata
250ml water
sea salt

Assemble all the ingredients and equipment before you begin. You need a large sauté or frying pan.

Remove and discard the prawn tails, if necessary. Lightly crush the cardamom pods to loosen the seeds. Rinse and chop enough coriander sprigs to make about 2 tablespoons and set aside a few sprigs for a garnish.

Heat the vegetable oil over a medium-high heat in the pan. Add the cardamom pods and the seeds, the cloves and fennel seeds, and stir until the spices crackle. Add the onion paste and stir it into the oil for 30 seconds. Add the ground coriander, chilli powder and passata. Season with salt and stir for 30 seconds–1 minute to cook the spices. The mixture will have a paste-like texture. Watch closely so the spices do not burn.

Add the chopped coriander, prawns and water. Bring to a simmering point, stirring for 30 seconds, or until the prawns turn pink. Adjust the seasoning with salt, if necessary. Garnish with coriander sprigs to serve.

Atul's time-saving tips

Buy raw prawns that have already been shelled, and this warming and satisfying curry will be on the table in less than 15 minutes. That's quicker than the time it takes to heat the oven and cook a ready meal. If the prawns need thawing, however, put them in a large colander or sieve and run lukewarm water over them until they thaw.

PRAWN AND COCONUT CURRY

Narkol Chengri Moli

Here's some almost-instant sunshine in a bowl from the Bengali coastal region.

SERVES 4

500g raw peeled tiger prawns (see Atul's tip, page 111)
3 green cardamom pods
fresh coriander leaves
1 tablespoon ghee or vegetable oil
2 cloves
1 dried bay leaf
1 cinnamon stick
1 tablespoon Onion Paste (page 218)
½ teaspoon red chilli powder, or to taste
¼ teaspoon ground turmeric
250ml coconut milk
sea salt

Assemble all the ingredients and equipment before you begin. You need a large sauté or frying pan with a lid.

Remove and discard the prawn tails, if necessary. Lightly crush the cardamom pods to loosen the seeds. Rinse and chop enough coriander leaves to make about 1 tablespoon.

Melt the ghee over a medium-high heat in the pan. Add the cardamom pods and the seeds, the cloves, bay leaf and cinnamon stick, and stir until the spices crackle. Add the onion paste and stir it into the oil for 30 seconds. Add the chilli powder and turmeric and stir for 30 seconds to cook the spices. Watch closely so they do not burn.

Reduce the heat to medium and add the prawns and coconut milk. Season with salt and continue stirring for 30 seconds, or until the prawns turn pink on both sides. Take care not to over-cook the prawns.

Adjust the seasoning with salt, if necessary, and stir in the chopped coriander just before serving.

PRAWN AND MANGO SALAD

Jhinga Aur Aam Ka Salad

This is more about preparation than cooking, but I love this salad so much I couldn't not include it. I picked up the recipe after discovering it being made on the street in Malaysia. I thought at the time I could put my own twist on it, and that's what I've done. In the summer, it's excellent with the prawns grilled on a barbecue.

I've included fish sauce in the dressing, but leave it out if you don't like it or want to keep the salad vegetarian, although I think it's quite an important condiment for a salad like this.

SERVES 2

1 green mango
1 tomato
½ banana shallot, or 1 ordinary
  shallot
1cm piece of fresh ginger
several small sprigs fresh coriander
25g raw unsalted peanuts
½ teaspoon dried chilli flakes, or
  to taste
2 tablespoons vegetable oil
120g raw peeled tiger prawns,
  without tails
sea salt

For the spice powder
½ teaspoon coriander seeds
½ teaspoon cumin seeds

For the dressing
1 lime
½ teaspoon sugar
½ teaspoon Thai fish sauce, or
  to taste (optional)

Assemble all the ingredients and equipment before you begin. You need a large bowl, another large non-reactive bowl, a pestle and mortar, a non-stick pan for toasting the spices, a spice grinder and a large sauté or frying pan.

Peel the mango, then thinly slice the flesh lengthways from both sides until you reach the central stone. Stack the slices and then cut into very thin julienne slices. Transfer to the large bowl.

Quarter the tomato, cut out the cores and seeds and thinly slice the flesh, then add to the bowl. Peel and halve the shallot, then slice it lengthways as thinly as possible and add it to the bowl.

Peel and very, very finely chop the ginger, then add it to the bowl. If you aren't confident about your chopping skills, it can be grated.

Rinse several small coriander sprigs and add the leaves to the bowl with the other salad ingredients.

Put the peanuts in the pestle and gently pound to crush, then tip them into the bowl. Add the chilli flakes. Gently toss the salad ingredients together and set aside.

To make the spice powder, heat the dry non-stick pan over a high heat. Add the coriander and cumin seeds and stir until they are aromatic. Tip the spices into a spice blender and grind until a coarse powder forms. Add to the bowl with the salad ingredients and set aside.

To make the dressing, squeeze the juice from the lime into the non-reactive bowl. Add the sugar and stir until it dissolves. Stir in the fish sauce to taste. Set aside.

Cook the prawns just before you are ready to serve. Heat the vegetable oil over a medium-high heat in the sauté pan. Add the prawns, season with salt and stir for 1–2 minutes until they are pink on both sides and curl.

continued on page 116

When the prawns are all cooked, add the dressing to the salad ingredients and toss together.

Transfer the salad to a serving bowl or platter and arrange the hot prawns on top.

Atul's time-saving tip
You can prepare all the salad ingredients and dressing in advance, ready to assemble, and then cook the prawns just before serving. Keep the mango, tomato and shallot in a covered container in the fridge and don't add the dressing until you cook the prawns.

MARINATED MACKEREL

Bhangra Masala

When it comes to quick-cooking, you can't go wrong with mackerel fillets. I've always included them in menus at home, not least of all because they are so good and simple to cook. These can be pan-fried, but here I want the simplicity of cooking them under the grill. To round out your meal, just make a simple tomato and lettuce salad.

I suggest leaving the mackerel fillets to only marinate for ten minutes, so this recipe is super-quick, but you can also leave them for up to twenty-four hours if you have time. The fragrant marinade also works well with sea bass and haddock fillets.

SERVES 4

1 lemon
2 tablespoons Benares Curry Powder (page 223)
2 teaspoons Ginger-Garlic Paste (page 220)
8 mackerel fillets, about 90g each
vegetable oil for brushing the grill rack
sea salt

Assemble all the ingredients and equipment before you begin. You need a non-reactive bowl and a grill rack.

Squeeze 2 tablespoons of lemon juice into the bowl. Add the curry powder and ginger-garlic paste and season with salt, then mix together. Spread this mixture over the flesh side of the fillets and set aside to marinate for at least 10 minutes.

Meanwhile, preheat the grill to high and brush the grill rack with oil.

Place the fillets, skin-side down, on the rack and position it about 3cm from the heat. Grill for 5–7 minutes until cooked through and the flesh flakes easily.

Atul's time-saving tip
Save yourself a lot of time washing up and line the grill pan with kitchen foil, shiny side up.

SQUID CURRY

Kunthal Kari

This is a simple fisherman-style curry, and you can use just about any other seafood you like, although I tend to avoid the oily fish, such as mackerel and herring.

SERVES 4

450g prepared squid
250ml Tamarind Liquid (page 223)
2 shallots
1 heaped tablespoon coconut oil
1 teaspoon black mustard seeds
15 fresh or dried curry leaves
½ teaspoon salt

For the spice paste

3 shallots
2cm piece of fresh ginger
2 teaspoons red chilli powder, or to taste
2 teaspoons ground coriander
100g desiccated coconut
½ teaspoon ground turmeric
6 tablespoons water

Assemble all the ingredients and equipment before you begin. You need a saucepan, food processor fitted with a chopping blade, a non-stick pan for toasting the spices and a large non-stick sauté or frying pan.

Slice the squid into 1cm rings and halve the tentacles. Put the squid and tamarind liquid in the saucepan and leave to simmer over a low heat, stirring occasionally.

Meanwhile, peel and halve the 3 shallots for the paste and peel, halve and thinly slice the remaining 2 shallots that will be in the curry. Set them aside separately. Peel and coarsely chop the ginger for the spice paste.

To make the spice paste, put the halved shallots and chopped ginger in the food processor and set aside. Put the chilli powder and ground coriander in the dry non-stick pan over a high heat and stir for 30 seconds. Watch closely so they do not burn. Transfer the spices to the food processor. Add the coconut, turmeric and water, and blitz, scraping down the sides of the bowl as necessary until a coarse paste forms. Set aside.

Melt the coconut oil over a medium-high heat in the non-stick sauté pan. Add the mustard seeds and stir until they pop. Add the thinly sliced shallots and curry leaves and stir until the shallots are softened, but not coloured. Add the spice paste and stir for a further 2 minutes.

Tip the spice mixture into the pan with the squid. Add the salt and simmer for 5 minutes, or until the squid is tender, and then serve.

GOAN FISH CURRY

Goa Peixe Kari

Typical of Goan curries, this is hot and spicy with a sour tang from tamarind, and it has thin gravy. I love the heat. It's just so beautiful.

Here I've pan-fried the sea bass fillet for a stylish, restaurant-style presentation, but if you want to turn this into a sharing curry to put in the centre of the table, cut the fish into bite-sized pieces and gently simmer them in the gravy until the flesh flakes easily. This quantity will then serve four to six people, and all you need with it is a bowl of basmati rice to complete the meal. Cod and pollack are other suitable fish to use, but they should simmer for just a bit longer.

SERVES 4

vegetable oil
2 tablespoons Onion Paste
   (page 218)
2 tablespoons canned chopped
   tomatoes
250ml coconut milk
2 tablespoons Tamarind Liquid (page
   223), or to taste
200ml water
1 long thin green chilli
4 large sea bass fillets, skin on
fresh coriander sprigs, to garnish
sea salt

For the spice powder

2 large dried red chillies
1 tablespoon coriander seeds
2 teaspoons cumin seeds
1 teaspoon ground turmeric

Assemble all the ingredients and equipment before you begin. You need a spice grinder, 2 sauté or frying pans, one of which is large and non-stick, and a baking tray.

First make the spice powder. Put the dried red chillies, coriander and cumin seeds and turmeric in the spice grinder, and grind until a fine powder forms. Set aside.

Heat 2 tablespoons of the vegetable oil over a medium-high heat in the sauté pan that isn't non-stick. Add the spice powder and stir for 30 seconds to cook the spices. Watch closely so they do not burn. Add the onion paste and stir for a further 30 seconds. Lower the heat to medium, add the tomatoes and continue stirring to break down the large chunks.

Stir in the coconut milk, tamarind liquid and water. Slit the green chilli lengthways, then add it to the pan. Season with salt and bring the liquid to the boil, then lower the heat and leave to simmer, uncovered and stirring occasionally, while you cook the fish. You want the gravy to have a consistency like single cream.

Meanwhile, rinse a few coriander sprigs for the garnish and set aside. Pat the fish fillets dry and cut each fillet in half crossways. Use a thin knife to lightly score the skin side of each fillet. Season with salt on the flesh side.

Heat just enough vegetable oil to cover the surface of the non-stick pan over a medium-high heat. Add the fillets, skin side down, and fry for 3–4 minutes until the skin is browned and crisp. Gently flip the fillets over and continue frying until the flesh is opaque and cooked through. Take care not to over-cook the fillets.

Adjust the seasoning of the gravy with salt, if necessary. Divide the gravy among 4 deep soup plates or bowls and top each with 2 pieces of sea bass. Garnish with the coriander sprigs.

Atul's time-saving tip

Lightly scoring the skin on the fillets helps them cook quicker and crisps the skin. This isn't just because I have my eye on the clock with these recipes, but because gentle, quick cooking guarantees tender, delicious results.

SEA BASS WITH SPINACH

Palakwali Machhi

Cardamom isn't a spice normally cooked with fish, but here I use both green and black cardamom seeds to flavour the spinach in this Kashmiri-inspired dish. I think the result is very successful. The spinach is also given an extra dimension with dried fenugreek leaves, which you can find in Indian food shops. I devised this recipe with 125g of spinach leaves per portion, but if you want more, please feel free to increase.

For variety, substitute 2½ teaspoons Benares Curry Powder (page 223) for the ground turmeric, red chilli powder and ground ginger and cinnamon.

SERVES 4

2.5cm piece of ginger
4 large sea bass fillets, skin on
1 tablespoon vegetable oil
sea salt
1 lemon, to garnish (optional)

For the spinach

500g baby spinach leaves
3 green cardamom pods
1 black cardamom pod
3 garlic cloves
1 onion
2 tablespoons vegetable oil
¼ teaspoon black cumin seeds, or use ordinary
1 teaspoon ground turmeric
½ teaspoon red chilli powder, or to taste
½ teaspoon ground ginger
¼ teaspoon ground cinnamon
2 tablespoons dried fenugreek leaves
½ lemon

Assemble all the ingredients and equipment before you begin. You need a colander or sieve, a pestle and mortar, a wok and a large non-stick sauté or frying pan.

First prepare the ingredients for the spinach. Rinse the spinach leaves and shake off the excess water. Lightly crush the green and black cardamom pods to remove the seeds, then grind the seeds with a pestle and mortar. Peel and thinly slice the garlic cloves. Peel, halve and thinly slice the onion.

To cook the spinach, heat the 2 tablespoons of vegetable oil over a medium-high heat in the wok. Add the garlic and black cumin seeds and stir until the seeds crackle. Add the onion with a pinch of salt and continue stirring until the onion is softened, but not coloured. Add the ground cardamom seeds, the turmeric, chilli powder, ginger and cinnamon, and continue stirring for 30 seconds to cook the spices. Watch closely so they do not burn.

Add the wet spinach a handful at a time, stirring and pressing it down until it all fits into the wok. Add the dried fenugreek leaves. Season with salt, increase the heat and continue stirring for 3–4 minutes until the spinach reduces in volume and is tender, but not reduced to a mush – you want to have some texture left. Squeeze in 1 tablespoon of lemon juice and reserve the lemon shell. Set the spinach aside and keep hot.

Peel the knob of ginger. Coarsely chop 2 or 3 small pieces, which will be used to flavour the oil used for cooking the fish, then thinly slice the remainder and cut into fine julienne slices to use as a garnish. Set aside separately.

Pat the fish fillets dry. Use a thin knife to slightly score the skin side of each fillet. Season lightly with salt on the flesh side, then set aside.

Heat the 1 tablespoon of vegetable oil over a medium-high heat in the sauté pan. Add the chopped ginger and stir just until it turns light brown to flavour the oil, then remove it immediately – if it browns too much, it will add a bitter flavour.

Add the fillets, skin side down, and fry for 3–4 minutes until the skin is browned and crisp. Gently flip the fillets over and squeeze the juice from the lemon shell into the oil and add the shell to the pan for extra flavour. Continue frying until the flesh is opaque and cooked through. Take care not to over-cook the fillets.

Meanwhile, reheat the spinach, if necessary, and adjust the seasoning with salt. Cut the lemon for the garnish into wedges and set aside

Serve the fillets, skin side up, on a mound of spinach. Garnish with the ginger slices and serve with lemon wedges alongside, if you like.

TAMARIND FISH

Imli Machhi

I use sea bass in this recipe, but cod, haddock, plaice or almost any other fish would work just as well. Just be sure to buy fillets with skin on one side and pat them very dry before you put them in the hot pan. As always, the cooking time will depend on the thickness, so watch closely so you don't over-cook the fish.

SERVES 4

8 large sea bass fillets, skin on
2 tablespoons vegetable oil
sea salt
coriander sprigs, to garnish

For the tamarind sauce
1 tablespoon vegetable oil
a pinch of ground asafoetida
1 small dried bay leaf
½ teaspoon cumin seeds
1 tablespoon ground cumin
1 teaspoon ground coriander
¾ teaspoon ground fennel
¼ teaspoon red chilli powder, or
    to taste
¼ teaspoon garam masala
¼ teaspoon ground ginger
¼ teaspoon ground turmeric
¼ teaspoon sea salt
a pinch of ground cinnamon
150ml Tamarind Liquid (page 223)
2 teaspoons sugar, or to taste

Assemble all the ingredients and equipment before you begin. You need a saucepan and a large non-stick sauté or frying pan.

First make the tamarind sauce. Heat the vegetable oil over a medium-high heat in the saucepan. Add the asafoetida and stir until it sizzles. Add the bay leaf and cumin seeds and continue stirring until the seeds crackle. Add the cumin, coriander, fennel, chilli powder, garam masala, ginger, turmeric, salt and cinnamon, and stir for 30 seconds to cook the spices. Watch closely so they do not burn. Stir in the tamarind liquid and leave the sauce to simmer and thicken while you fry the fish, stirring occasionally.

Pat the fish fillets dry and season lightly with salt on the flesh side.

Heat the vegetable oil over a medium heat in the sauté pan. Add the fillets, flesh side down, and fry for 3 minutes, then gently turn over and fry until the skin is browned and crisp. The flesh should be opaque and cooked through. Take care not to over-cook the fillets.

Meanwhile, rinse a few coriander sprigs for a garnish and set aside.

Drain off the oil in the frying pan and return all the fillets to the pan. Taste the sauce and adjust the flavour with the sugar. Carefully pour the sauce into the pan and spoon over the fish. Serve the fillets garnished with coriander sprigs.

Atul's time-saving tip
One of the great things about this recipe is that the sauce can be made well in advance, if you like, ready for heating to serve with the freshly cooked fish at the very last minute. With the amount of tamarind and sugar the sauce contains, it should keep in a covered container in the fridge almost indefinitely.

MANGALOREAN FISH CURRY

Jalacara Kari

Developing this recipe was an absolute triumph. I'd never cooked anything like this before, and I loved the result. I am so enjoying this process.

I'm taking you on a bit of a journey here, down south along coastal India. We're in the state of Karnataka, where Mangalore is the largest culinary region. This is a very common fish curry of the region, much like a fisherman's fish supper. If you can't find the frozen grated coconut you could use desiccated coconut, but I'm not a great fan of it at all. A far better substitution is to replace the water in the spice paste with the same amount of coconut milk.

SERVES 4

2 tomatoes
1 onion
2 tablespoons vegetable oil
1 teaspoon black mustard seeds
12 fresh or dried curry leaves
375ml water
4 large sea bass fillets, skin on
sea salt

For the spice paste

5 garlic cloves
175ml water
50g frozen grated coconut
1 teaspoon coriander seeds
1 teaspoon cumin seeds
¼ teaspoon black peppercorns
a pinch fenugreek seeds

Assemble all the ingredients and equipment before you begin. You will need a food processor fitted with a chopping blade and a large sauté or frying pan.

First make the spice paste. Peel the garlic cloves and put them in a food processor. Add the water, frozen coconut, coriander and cumin seeds, peppercorns and fenugreek seeds to the food processor, and blitz, scraping down the sides of the bowl as necessary, until a gritty paste forms. It won't be smooth, and that is the character of the cuisine from this part of India. Set aside.

Halve and thinly slice the tomatoes. Peel, halve and thinly slice the onion.

Heat the vegetable oil over a medium-high heat in the pan. Add the mustard seeds and stir until they pop. Add the onion, curry leaves and a pinch of salt, and stir occasionally until the onion is softened, but not coloured.

Turn the heat to medium. Add the spice paste and stir for 30 seconds–1 minute to cook out the raw flavour. The oil will be absorbed and the liquid will evaporate. Add the tomatoes and water and stir into the onion mixture.

Turn up the heat and bring the mixture to the boil, stirring. Reduce the heat and leave the mixture to simmer, stirring occasionally, while you prepare the fish.

Cut each sea bass fillet into bite-sized pieces and season with salt.

Add the sea bass pieces to the curry mixture and leave them to simmer, gently stirring and turning the pieces over, for 3–4 minutes until the flesh flakes easily. Adjust the seasoning with salt, if necessary, and serve.

TAMIL FISH CURRY

Meen Kuzhambu

The flavours I've used in this curry are similar to those of English curry powder, and what I think most people think of as those in a Madras curry. This is full-flavoured and robust.

SERVES 4

1 tablespoon coconut oil
½ teaspoon cumin seeds
½ teaspoon fennel seeds
¼ teaspoon fenugreek seeds
10 fresh or dried curry leaves
1 tablespoon ground coriander
1 teaspoon red chilli powder, or
   to taste
200ml water
4 tablespoons Tamarind Liquid
   (page 223)
400g cod fillet or boneless haddock
   loin, in 2 pieces, skin on
vegetable oil
sea salt
1 lime, to garnish

For the spice paste

10 garlic cloves
2 tablespoons coconut oil
a pinch of black peppercorns
1 tablespoon fennel seeds
½ teaspoon cumin seeds
50g desiccated coconut
6 tablespoons canned chopped
   tomatoes
2 tablespoons Onion Paste
   (page 218)
200ml water

Assemble all the ingredients and equipment before you begin. You need a food processor fitted with a chopping blade and 2 sauté or frying pans, one of which is large and non-stick.

First make the spice paste. Peel the garlic cloves and crush them with the flat side of a large knife or the back of a wooden spoon, then coarsely chop. Melt the oil over a medium-high heat in the pan that isn't non-stick. Add the peppercorns and fennel and cumin seeds, and stir until the spices crackle. Reduce the heat to low, add the chopped garlic and coconut and stir until the coconut absorbs the oil.

Add the tomatoes and onion paste and continue stirring for 30 seconds to mix together. Stir in the water. Transfer the mixture to the food processor and blitz until well combined, scraping down the sides of the bowl as necessary. Set aside. Wash and dry the pan.

Melt the 1 tablespoon of coconut oil over a medium-high heat in the cleaned pan. Add the cumin, fennel and fenugreek seeds, and stir until the cumin and fennel seeds crackle and the fenugreek seeds turn darker. Stir in the curry leaves, ground coriander and chilli powder, and stir for 30 seconds to cook the spices. Watch closely so they do not burn.

Add the spice paste – stand well back because there will be lots of steam – water and tamarind liquid, and continue stirring for about 2 minutes. Season with salt, turn the heat to low and leave to simmer, stirring occasionally, while you prepare the fish.

Meanwhile, cut each piece of fish into 6 chunks, pat dry and season with salt on the flesh side. Cut the lime for the garnish into wedges and set aside.

Heat enough vegetable oil to cover the bottom of the non-stick pan over a medium-high heat. Add the fish pieces, skin side down, and fry for 3–4 minutes until the skins are browned and crisp. Gently turn the fish over and continue frying until the flesh is opaque and cooked through. The exact time will depend on the thickness of the fish you use, but take care not to over-cook.

To serve, pool the gravy in the centre of 4 plates and add 3 pieces of fish, skin side up, to each plate. Add a wedge of lime to each plate.

Atul's time-saving tip

For speed and variety you can poach the fish pieces in the curry mixture, as in the Mangalorean Fish Curry (page 126), rather than pan-frying.

KERALA FISH CURRY

Nadan Meen Mappas

The flavours in this recipe are spectacular. Kerala is the only part of India where you will find seafood cooked with cardamom, cinnamon and black pepper, quite simply because these spices grow in abundance there.

This is one of the recipes I put on my restaurant menus time and time again. You can make this with almost any fish you want – lobster, squid and prawns are particularly good – but I advise against mackerel, which is too oily and I don't think it goes well. I also recommend serving with rice to soak up the rich and fragrant gravy. I could have made this with onion paste to save time, but the texture of the onions is a particular characteristic of this curry.

SERVES 4

4 green cardamom pods
1 long thin green chilli
1 onion
1 tablespoon coconut oil
4 cloves
5cm piece of cinnamon stick
10 fresh or dried curry leaves
2 teaspoons Ginger-Garlic Paste
   (page 220)
½ teaspoon ground black pepper
½ teaspoon ground turmeric
400ml coconut milk
150ml water
4 fish fillets, 90–100g each, such as
   sea bass, sea bream, pollock or
   whiting, skin on
½ lime
sea salt

Assemble all the ingredients and equipment before you begin. You need a large non-stick sauté or frying pan.

Lightly crush the cardamom pods to loosen the seeds. Remove the stalk from the chilli, if necessary, then cut the chilli in half lengthways. Peel, halve and thinly slice the onion.

Melt the coconut oil over a medium-high heat in the pan. Add the cardamom pods and the seeds, the cloves and cinnamon, and stir until the spices crackle. Add the green chilli, onion and curry leaves, and continue stirring until the onion is just lightly coloured.

Turn the heat to medium. Add the ginger-garlic paste and stir it into the oil for 30 seconds. Add the black pepper and turmeric and stir for a further 30 seconds to cook the spices. Watch closely so they do not burn.

Stir in the coconut milk and water. Season with salt and bring to the boil. Lower the heat and leave the gravy to simmer, uncovered, while you prepare the fish.

Cut each fish fillet into 4cm slices and season with salt. Stir them directly into the curry and leave to simmer, uncovered, for 3–4 minutes until the flesh flakes easily. Take care not to over-cook the thin pieces.

Squeeze 1 teaspoon of lime juice into the curry to cut through the richness and adjust the seasoning with salt, if necessary, then divide the sauce among 4 plates or bowls and serve.

BENGALI FISH CURRY

Macher Jhol

I don't think many Bengali cooks would add lime juice to a fish curry, but recipes are all about taste, flavours and textures, and I think a small amount works really well in this dish.

SERVES 4

4 large fish fillets, such as sea bass, pollock or whiting, skin on
½ teaspoon red chilli powder, or to taste
1½ teaspoons ground turmeric
1 long thin green chilli
1 small onion
2 tablespoons mustard oil
1 dried bay leaf
1 large dried red chilli
½ teaspoon black mustard seeds
½ teaspoon onion seeds
1 tablespoon Onion Paste (page 218)
1½ teaspoons ground coriander
¼ teaspoon red chilli powder, or to taste
350ml water
1 teaspoon Dijon mustard
½ lime
vegetable oil
fresh coriander leaves
sea salt

Assemble all the ingredients and equipment before you begin. You need a non-reactive bowl, 2 large sauté or frying pans, one of which is non-stick, and a plate.

Use a thin knife to lightly score the skin side of each fillet, with the scores about 1cm apart, then cut the fillets into 5cm pieces. Put the fish in the bowl, add the chilli powder, 1 teaspoon of the turmeric and a good pinch of salt, and mix together with a spoon so the pieces are well coated in spices. Set aside to marinate while you prepare the other ingredients.

Remove the stalk from the green chilli, if necessary, then cut the chilli in half lengthways. Peel, quarter and thinly slice the onion.

Heat the mustard oil over a medium-high heat in the pan that isn't non-stick. Add the bay leaf, red chilli and mustard and onion seeds, and stir until the mustard seeds pop and the onion seeds crackle. Add the onion with a pinch of salt and continue stirring until it is softened, but not coloured. Add the onion paste and stir it into the oil for 30 seconds. Add the green chilli and continue stirring, making sure nothing catches on the bottom of the pan.

Add the ground coriander, chilli powder and remaining the turmeric and stir for 30 seconds to cook the spices. Stir in the water and mustard. Season with salt and squeeze in 1 tablespoon of lime juice, then leave the gravy to simmer over a medium heat while you fry the fish.

Heat enough vegetable oil to thinly cover the bottom of the non-stick pan over a high heat. Add the pieces of fish coated in the spices, skin side down, and fry for 2–3 minutes until the skin is browned. Watch closely so the spices do not burn.

Meanwhile, rinse and chop enough coriander leaves to make about 2 tablespoons.

When the skins are crisp, turn the fillets over and fry for a minute or so to seal. Transfer the pieces of fish to the pan with the gravy, reduce the heat and leave to simmer just until the flesh is opaque and cooked through. Take care not to over-cook the thin pieces. Adjust the seasoning with salt, if necessary, and stir in the chopped coriander.

HYDERABADI SOUR FISH

Khatti Machhi

This is a very simple recipe, and one of the quickest to cook in the book. I've deliberately left the skin on the sea bass fillets. I know a lot of cooks would be tempted to remove the skin, but I enjoy eating fish with the skin, and it saves you time when preparing the ingredients.

In Hindi, *khatti* means 'sour', and the sharpness of this recipe comes from the tomatoes and a little lemon juice.

SERVES 4

4 large sea bass fillets, skin on
1 lemon
2 tablespoons Ginger-Garlic Paste (page 220)
½ teaspoon red chilli powder, or to taste
1 teaspoon ground turmeric
vegetable oil
¼ teaspoon fenugreek seeds
350ml passata
10 fresh or dried curry leaves
sea salt
fresh coriander sprigs, to garnish

Assemble all the ingredients and equipment before you begin. You need a non-reactive bowl, a saucepan and a large non-stick sauté or frying pan.

Cut the fillets in half, then place them in the bowl. Squeeze in 2 tablespoons of lemon juice and add the ginger-garlic paste, chilli powder and turmeric. Season with salt and use a spoon to gently stir together so all the pieces are well coated with the paste-like marinade. Set aside to marinate while you prepare the gravy.

Heat 1 tablespoon of the vegetable oil over a medium-high heat in the saucepan. Add the fenugreek seeds and fry until they become darker in colour. Add the passata and curry leaves. Season with salt, reduce the heat to medium and leave the gravy to simmer while you fry the fish.

Heat enough vegetable oil to thinly cover the bottom of the frying pan over a high heat. Add the fillets coated in the marinade, skin side down, and fry for 2 minutes, or until the skin is browned.

Turn the fillets over and reduce the heat to medium. Pour the gravy into the pan around the fillets and leave to simmer until the flesh is opaque and cooked through. Take care not to over-cook them. Adjust the seasoning with salt, if necessary. Garnish with coriander sprigs and serve.

Atul's time-saving tip
If I hadn't included passata in this recipe, it would have been necessary to blanch, peel and de-seed the tomatoes before puréeing and sieving them. This is a much quicker way to achieve the sour tomato gravy.

FISH TAWA MASALA

Machhi Tawa Masala

I absolutely love cooking this dish. It's a colourful, domestic version of Punjabi street food, and it takes its title from the *tawa*, a flat griddle used to cook the fish. I serve this family style – I put the pepper mixture on a platter, top with the succulent pieces of fish and put it in the centre of the table for everyone to help themselves. It's good served with bread.

One of the reasons I like this dish so much is because the combination of anjowan seeds and garlic is, to my mind, unbeatable. Anjowan come from the celery family and have a slightly aniseed flavour, but not at all like fennel. You can get the seeds from any good Indian food supplier. If you don't have any, however, caraway seeds are a good substitute.

Hake is a hugely undervalued fish in Britain. I love, love, love this fish, and as time goes by I use more and more of it in my cooking. It's wild and sustainable, and you can buy the farmed variety. Hake is a particularly good match for this pepper mixture, but any firm white fish works, so feel free to use cod or haddock if you'd rather.

SERVES 4

3 garlic cloves
1 onion
vegetable oil
1 teaspoon anjowan seeds
1 green pepper
1 red pepper
1 yellow pepper
2 tomatoes
1½ teaspoons ground coriander
¾ teaspoon garam masala
½ teaspoon red chilli powder, or to taste
½ teaspoon ground turmeric
¼ teaspoon ground fenugreek
2 tablespoons Onion Masala (page 222)
125ml water
500g hake fillet in one piece, skin on
fresh coriander leaves
sea salt

Assemble all the ingredients and equipment before you begin. You need 2 large sauté or frying pans, one with a lid and one that is non-stick.

Peel and finely chop the garlic cloves. Peel, halve and thinly slice the onion.

Heat 2 tablespoons of the vegetable oil in the pan with a lid over a medium-high heat. Add ½ teaspoon of the anjowan seeds and stir until they crackle. Add the garlic and stir for 30 seconds to flavour the oil. Add the onion with a pinch of salt, reduce the heat slightly and stir occasionally until it is softened, but not coloured.

Meanwhile, halve and quarter the peppers. Remove and discard the cores and seeds, then thinly slice the flesh. Increase the heat under the pan, add the peppers with a pinch of salt and stir for 1½ minutes. Cover the pan and leave the pan over a medium-high heat until the peppers are beginning to soften.

While the peppers are softening, halve and slice the tomatoes. There isn't any need to de-seed them.

Add the ground coriander, ¼ teaspoon of the garam masala, the chilli powder, turmeric and fenugreek to the pan with the peppers, and stir for 30 seconds to cook the spices.

Add the tomatoes and onion masala to the pan and stir for 30 seconds, then stir in the water. Re-cover the pan, turn the heat to medium and leave

continued on page 138

everything to simmer, stirring occasionally, until the peppers soften and the tomatoes break down to form a 'thickish' gravy.

While the peppers and tomatoes are cooking, cut the hake into pieces about 1cm thick. Pat them dry with kitchen paper, then season with salt. Rinse and finely chop enough coriander leaves to make about 2 tablespoons.

Stir the remaining ½ teaspoon of the anjowan seeds and remaining ½ of the teaspoon garam masala into the pepper and tomato mixture. Re-cover the pan and leave to continue simmering over a medium-low heat while you cook the fish.

Heat enough vegetable oil to thinly cover the bottom of the non-stick pan over a high heat. Add the hake pieces, skin-side down, and fry for 2–3 minutes until the skins are browned. Gently turn the pieces over and continue frying until the flesh is opaque and cooked through. Take care not to over-cook the pieces of fish.

Adjust the seasoning of the gravy with salt, if necessary, and stir in about three-quarters of the chopped coriander. Transfer the pepper mixture to a large platter, top with the pieces of fish and sprinkle with the remaining coriander, just before serving.

PUNJABI FISH CURRY

Machhi Curry

I absolutely love and enjoy cooking fish. There is nothing that gives me more satisfaction than fish cookery, and I can't tell you how much I enjoy making fish curry with fish that has a bit of texture, because often it seems to be made with fish that disintegrates into the curry. I think this is most likely because of my upbringing in India, where we used kingfish, a mackerel that holds its shape beautifully. I've used hake fillet here, but other fish that are ideal include cod, haddock, monkfish and pollock. I would serve this with plain boiled rice.

For many of the recipes throughout this book I encourage you to have a good supply of Onion Masala (page 222) in the fridge or freezer for adding flavour and richness to a dish quickly. It's a regular feature of my cooking at home or in the restaurants. If you don't have any, however, I think you can still achieve this dish within the thirty-minute limit if you use tomato chutney or a little extra passata and double the quantity of spices.

SERVES 4

1 long thin green chilli
½ onion
vegetable oil
¼ teaspoon ground asafoetida
1 teaspoon cumin seeds
2 tablespoons Onion Masala
  (page 222)
1 teaspoon ground coriander
¼ teaspoon red chilli powder
¼ teaspoon ground turmeric
4 tablespoons passata
250ml water
500g hake fillet in one piece, skin on
½ lemon
fresh coriander leaves
sea salt

Assemble all the ingredients and equipment before you begin. You need 2 large sauté or frying pans, one of which is non-stick with a lid.

Remove the stalk from the green chilli, if necessary, then cut the chilli in half lengthways. Peel and thinly slice the onion.

Heat 1 tablespoon of the vegetable oil over a medium-high heat in the pan without a lid. Add the asafoetida and stir until it sizzles. Add the cumin seeds and fry until they crackle. Add the onion with a pinch of salt and stir until it is softened, but not coloured.

Add the onion masala and stir for 30 seconds to incorporate it into the onions and blend the flavours. Stir in the ground coriander, chilli powder and turmeric, and continue stirring for 30 seconds. Watch closely so the spices do not burn.

Add the passata and stir for a further 30 seconds. Add the green chilli halves and the water, then leave the gravy to simmer, uncovered, over a medium heat.

Meanwhile, cut the hake fillet into twelve 2.5cm slices. Pat the slices dry with kitchen paper and season with salt.

Heat enough oil to thinly cover the bottom of the non-stick pan with a lid over a high heat. Add the hake pieces, skin side down, and fry for 2 minutes to brown the skin. Gently turn the pieces over and continue frying for a further 1 minute to seal. Pour the gravy around the fish, but not over

continued on page 140

it, then cover the pan, reduce the heat to medium and leave to simmer for a minute or so to blend the flavours and until the flesh is opaque and cooked through. Take care not to over-cook the pieces.

While the fish is simmering, squeeze 1 tablespoon of lemon juice. Rinse and chop enough coriander leaves to make about 1 tablespoon.

Stir the lemon juice into the gravy. Adjust the seasoning with salt, if necessary, and stir in about three-quarters of the chopped coriander. Transfer the curry to a serving bowl and sprinkle with the remaining coriander.

HYDERABADI FISH CURRY

Machhi Ka Salan

Hyderabadi cooks use freshwater fish for this recipe, such as carp, but any firm white fish is good. I serve this with boiled rice.

SERVES 4

1 tablespoon vegetable oil

3 tablespoons Onion Paste (page 218)

4 tablespoons Tamarind Liquid (page 223)

125ml passata

125ml coconut milk

125ml water

1 large fish fillet, such as salmon, sea bass and sea bream, skin on

sea salt

fresh coriander sprigs, to garnish

For the spice powder

1 tablespoon coriander seeds

2 teaspoons red chilli powder, or to taste

1 teaspoon cumin seeds

1 teaspoon ground turmeric

Assemble all the ingredients and equipment before you begin. You need a spice grinder and a large sauté or frying pan.

First make the spice powder. Put the coriander seeds, chilli powder, cumin seeds and turmeric in the spice grinder, and grind until a fine powder forms. Set aside.

Heat the vegetable oil over a medium-high heat in the pan. Add the onion paste and stir it into the oil for 30 seconds. Add the spice powder and tamarind liquid and stir for 30 seconds to cook the spices. Watch closely so they do not burn.

Add the passata and stir to cook through. Stir in the coconut milk and water. Season with salt and bring to the boil, stirring. Leave to gently bubble, uncovered, while you prepare the fish.

Cut the fish fillet into 4cm slices and season with salt. Gently stir them into the curry. Reduce the heat to medium and leave to simmer, uncovered and turning the fish pieces over once or twice, for 3–4 minutes until the flesh is cooked through and opaque. Take care not to over-cook them.

Meanwhile, rinse the coriander sprigs for garnishing and set aside.

Adjust the seasoning with salt, if necessary, and garnish with coriander sprigs to serve.

MAMAK FISH CURRY

Kari Ikan Mamak

Mamaks are the people who moved from India to Malaysia, so this curry is a blend of two cuisines. I've used salmon, but you can also use any meaty white fish. Monkfish would be ideal, but it's expensive, and cod or haddock work just as well. In India, I would definitely use kingfish.

SERVES 4

500g thick salmon fillet
8 okra pods
10 cherry or small plum tomatoes
1 tablespoon vegetable oil
10 fresh or dried curry leaves
½ teaspoon panch phoron
1 tablespoon Onion Paste
    (page 218)
½ teaspoon ground turmeric
250ml water
3 tablespoons Tamarind Liquid
    (page 223)
125ml coconut milk
fresh coriander leaves
sea salt

For the spice powder
1 large dried red chilli
1 cinnamon stick
1 star anise
1 tablespoon coriander seeds
1 teaspoon fennel seeds
½ teaspoon cumin seeds
¼ teaspoon fenugreek seeds

Assemble all the ingredients and equipment before you begin. You need a non-stick pan for toasting the spices, a spice grinder and a large sauté or frying pan with a lid.

First make the spice powder. Heat the dry non-stick pan over a high heat. Add the dried chilli, cinnamon stick, star anise and coriander, fennel, cumin and fenugreek seeds, and stir until they are aromatic and toasted. Tip the spices into the spice grinder and grind until a fine powder forms. Set aside.

Remove any pin bones from the salmon, then cut the flesh into large bite-sized pieces. Trim the stalk ends from the okra pods, without cutting into the pods so they remain whole. Cut the cherry tomatoes in half.

Heat the vegetable oil over a medium-high heat in the sauté pan. Add the curry leaves and panch phoron and stir until the spices sizzle. Add the onion paste and stir it into the oil for 30 seconds. Add the spice powder and turmeric and stir for a further 30 seconds to cook the turmeric. Watch closely so the spices do not burn.

Add the water and 2 tablespoons of the tamarind liquid, bring to the boil and stir for 5 minutes, or until the liquid almost evaporates. Stir in the coconut milk.

Add the okra and tomatoes, cover the pan and leave to boil for 6–8 minutes until the okra is very tender, but the tomatoes are still whole.

Reduce the heat to medium and add the salmon with the remaining 1 tablespoon of tamarind liquid. Season with salt and leave to simmer, uncovered and turning the salmon occasionally, for 5 minutes, or until the flesh flakes easily.

Meanwhile, rinse and finely chop enough coriander leaves to make about 2 tablespoons.

Adjust the seasoning with salt, if necessary, and sprinkle with the chopped coriander to serve.

POULTRY

CHICKEN MEATBALLS

Murgh Kofta Curry

Inspired by Kashmiri recipes, the combination of garlic, fresh coriander and garam masala gives this chicken mixture a lovely aroma as you are mixing it. I then lighten and enrich the mixture with the addition of a little double cream.

SERVES 4

2 green cardamom pods
3 garlic cloves
a handful of fresh coriander sprigs
500g minced chicken
1 tablespoon ground coriander
1 tablespoon ground cumin
2 teaspoons garam masala
2 tablespoons double cream
sea salt

For the gravy
a large pinch of saffron threads
1 tablespoon warm water
fresh coriander leaves
6 cardamom pods
2 tablespoons vegetable oil
3 cloves
6 tablespoons Onion Paste
   (page 218)
1 lemon

Bring a covered saucepan of water, large enough to hold 12 meatballs, to the boil and assemble all the ingredients and other equipment before you begin. You also need a small bowl to infuse the saffron in, a pestle and mortar, a food processor fitted with a chopping blade, a mixing bowl, a small bowl of water, a slotted spoon, a large plate and a large sauté or frying pan with a lid.

Put the saffron and warm water for the gravy in the small bowl and set aside to infuse.

Use the pestle and mortar to finely crush the 2 cardamom pods, then set aside. Peel the garlic cloves and put them in the food processor. Rinse the fresh coriander, then roughly chop the leaves and stalks, add to the food processor and blitz until the garlic is finely chopped. Add the minced chicken, ground coriander, ground cumin, garam masala, cream and crushed cardamom pods and their seeds. Season with salt and process until blended, but still slightly coarse, scraping down the sides of the bowl as necessary.

Transfer the mixture to the mixing bowl. Use the bowl of water to wet your fingers and shape the chicken mixture into 12 equal meatballs.

Gently add the meatballs to the boiling water. Return the water to the boil and when the meatballs have risen to the surface, reduce the temperature to a simmer and poach for 5 minutes. Use the slotted spoon to transfer them to the plate, reserving the poaching liquid.

Meanwhile, to make the gravy, finely chop enough coriander leaves to make 2 tablespoons and lightly crush the 6 cardamom pods to loosen the seeds.

Heat the vegetable oil in the sauté pan over a medium-high heat. Add the cardamom pods and their seeds and the cloves and stir until they crackle. Add the onion paste and stir into the oil for 30 seconds. Add the saffron and its soaking liquid and 450ml of the meatball poaching water, and bring to the boil, stirring.

Reduce the heat, add the meatballs and stir until they are coated. Season with salt and leave to simmer for about 5 minutes.

While the mixture is simmering, squeeze 1½ tablespoons of lemon juice into the gravy to balance the flavours and stir in half the chopped coriander. Adjust the seasoning with salt, if necessary.

Divide the meatballs and sauce among 4 bowls and sprinkle with the remaining chopped coriander just before serving.

CHICKEN WITH CORIANDER AND SPINACH CHUTNEY

Hari Chutney Murgh

From the Mumbai region of Maharashtra, this dish has lots of beautiful, fresh flavours.

SERVES 4

4 part-boned chicken breasts
4 green cardamom pods
2 black cardamom pods
1 tablespoon vegetable oil
2 cloves
1 dried bay leaf
1 cinnamon stick
2 tablespoons Onion Paste (page 218)
4 tablespoons coconut milk
4 tablespoons Tamarind Liquid (page 223), or to taste
1 teaspoon garam masala
sea salt

For the coriander and spinach chutney

5cm piece of fresh ginger
2 long thin green chillies
50g fresh coriander sprigs
50g baby spinach leaves
125ml water

Assemble all the ingredients and equipment before you begin. You need a cleaver or large chef's knife, a large sauté or frying pan with a lid and a food processor fitted with chopping blade.

Get the chicken prepared and cooking as quickly as possible. (Buying skinned and chopped chicken pieces from a butcher will save time, but the important thing is to get pieces all from the same part of the bird, so they all cook at the same time. If you just chop up a whole bird, unfortunately, the breast pieces will be over-cooked by the time the thigh and leg pieces are ready.) Remove the skin from the chicken breasts, then chop them into bite-sized pieces, leaving the bones in. Lightly crush the green and black cardamom pods to loosen the seeds.

Heat the vegetable oil over a medium-high heat in the pan. Add the cardamom pods and their seeds, the cloves, bay leaf and cinnamon stick, and stir until the spices crackle. Add the onion paste and stir it into the oil for 30 seconds.

Add the chicken pieces. Season with salt and continue stirring until the pieces start to colour on all sides. Leave the chicken pieces to continue cooking over a medium-high heat, stirring occasionally and adding a few tablespoons of water, if necessary, to prevent the paste sticking to the pan.

Meanwhile, make the chutney. Peel and coarsely chop the ginger, then put it in the food processor. Remove the stalks from the green chillies, if necessary, then tear the chillies into the food processor. Rinse and shake dry the coriander and spinach leaves, then place both in the food processor. Add the water, season with salt and blitz, scraping down the sides of the bowl, as necessary, until a thin green paste forms.

Stir the coconut milk and 2 tablespoons of the tamarind liquid into the pan with the chicken, then add half the chutney, stirring until all the chicken pieces are coated. Season with salt, cover the pan and leave the curry to gently boil over a medium heat for 8–10 minutes, stirring occasionally, until all the chicken is tender and cooked through.

Stir in the remaining green chutney, the garam masala and the remaining 2 tablespoons of tamarind liquid to taste. Simmer for a further minute for all the flavours to blend. Adjust the seasoning with salt, if necessary.

MANGO AND CHICKEN CURRY

Kairi Ka Murgh

When I was preparing the green mangoes for this recipe, the aroma took me straight back to my schoolboy days. Friends and I would throw stones at the mangoes and tamarinds hanging from trees to land them for our after-school treat. I used to steal salt from my mum's kitchen, wrap it in a piece of tissue and keep it in my pocket just for such an opportunity. It's that beautiful combination of extremely sour and salty that I set out to re-create here.

Green mangoes are available all year round from Asian food shops.

SERVES 4

600g chicken thigh fillets
½ teaspoon red chilli powder, or to taste, plus a little extra to garnish
1 teaspoon ground turmeric
10 fresh or dried curry leaves
2 long thin green chillies
2 tablespoons vegetable oil
2 tablespoons water
3 small green mangoes
2 tablespoons Onion Paste (page 218)
½ teaspoon garam masala
fresh coriander leaves
sea salt

Assemble all the ingredients and equipment before you begin. You need a non-reactive bowl and a large sauté or frying pan with a lid.

Cut the chicken into bite-sized pieces. Put the chicken in the bowl with the chilli powder and turmeric, then season with salt and stir together so the chicken pieces are coated in spices. Roughly chop or crumble the curry leaves and stir them into the chicken, then set aside.

Remove the stalks from the green chillies, if necessary, then cut each chilli into 3 pieces.

Heat the vegetable oil over a medium-high heat in the pan. Add the chicken pieces with the curry leaves and stir for 2 minutes until the chicken changes colour. Watch closely so the spices on the chicken do not burn. Stir in the water, cover the pan and leave the chicken pieces to simmer over a medium heat while you prepare the mangoes.

Peel the mangoes, then cut them in half and use your fingers or a sharp knife to remove the white seed, then use a small spoon to scrape out the bitter white pith in the indentation where the seed was. Finely chop the flesh of 2 of the mangoes. Cut the flesh of the third mango into very fine julienne slices to use as a garnish.

Turn the heat under the pan with the chicken to medium-high. Add the chopped mangoes and onion paste and stir for 30 seconds. Stir in the green chillies and garam masala and season with salt. Reduce the heat to medium, re-cover the pan and leave the chicken and mangoes to cook for a further 5–7 minutes until the chicken is cooked through and tender.

Meanwhile, rinse and chop enough coriander leaves to make about 2 tablespoons. Stir three-quarters of the coriander into the curry and adjust the seasoning with salt, if necessary.

Sprinkle with the remaining chopped coriander and garnish with the raw mango slices and a sprinkling of chilli powder just before serving.

MANGALOREAN CHICKEN CURRY

Koli Kari

This curry is from the port city of Mangalore, in southwest India. The beauty of this coastal area is that it has a lot of Catholic people living there, so they eat beef and pork, along with the other meats. The flavours are pretty robust in character and slightly more powerful than in some other regions, because the spices are slightly stronger.

If you have any leftovers, you will have to add a bit more liquid while reheating, because the coconut will have absorbed all the liquid.

SERVES 4

600g chicken thigh fillets
1 onion
2 tablespoons coconut oil
1 teaspoon black mustard seeds
10 fresh or dried curry leaves, plus extra fresh to garnish (optional)
1½ teaspoons red chilli powder, or to taste
250ml coconut milk
1 lemon
sea salt

For the spice paste

8 garlic cloves
8 black peppercorns
3 green cardamom pods
1 dried red chilli
4cm piece of cinnamon stick
1 tablespoon coriander seeds
1 teaspoon cumin seeds
250ml water
175g frozen grated coconut
15 fresh or dried curry leaves
2 tablespoons Onion Paste (page 218)

Assemble all the ingredients before you begin. You need a spice grinder, a food processor fitted with a chopping blade and a large sauté or frying pan.

First make the spice paste. Peel the garlic cloves and set aside. Put the peppercorns, cardamom pods, dried chilli, cinnamon stick and coriander and cumin seeds in the spice grinder, and grind until a fine powder forms. Tip the powder into the food processor, add the garlic cloves, water, frozen coconut, curry leaves and onion paste, and blitz until a smooth paste forms. Set aside.

Cut the chicken into bite-sized pieces. Peel, halve and thinly slice the onion.

Melt the coconut oil over a medium-high heat in the sauté pan. Add the mustard seeds and stir until they pop. Watch closely, because coconut oil has a low smoking point, but you need it to be quite hot for the mustard seeds to pop. Stir in the onions and curry leaves. Season with salt and continue stirring until the onions are softened, but not coloured. Add the spice paste, turn the heat up and continue stirring for about 2 minutes to cook all the ingredients in the paste. The raw garlic smell should disappear as you cook.

Add the chicken pieces and stir until they are coated with the paste. Stir in the chilli powder and continue stirring for 30 seconds to cook the chilli powder. Watch closely so it does not burn. Add the coconut milk and bring to the boil, stirring. Turn the heat to medium and leave the curry to bubble, uncovered, while you squeeze about 2 tablespoons of lemon juice.

Stir the lemon juice into the curry and leave it to continue gently bubbling for 8–10 minutes, or until the chicken is cooked through and tender. Adjust the seasoning with salt, if necessary. Add a curry leaf or two just before serving if you have fresh ones.

FENUGREEK CHICKEN CU[RRY]

Kasoori Kukkar

The best fenugre[ek]
Kasur, in Pakista[n]
dark curry. This [i]
think anyone in I[n]
on, but they add
as the thighs finis[h]
the beautiful taste. [I]
thighs to an oven preh[eated to]
cooking and then serve ther

SERVES 4

4 chicken thighs, about 150g each,
   skin on
3 tablespoons vegetable oil
5cm piece of fresh ginger
1 onion
4 green cardamom pods
5 black peppercorns
1 teaspoon cumin seeds
6 tablespoons Onion Paste
   (page 218)
1 tablespoon ground coriander
1 teaspoon red chilli powder, or to
   taste
1 teaspoon ground turmeric
500ml water
5 tablespoons passata
1 dried bay leaf
2 teaspoons dried fenugreek
   leaf powder
1 teaspoon garam masala
fresh coriander leaves
sea salt

Assemble all the ingredients before
you begin. You need 2 large sauté
or frying pans, one of which is
ideally non-stick and the other with
a lid. A splatter guard large enough
to cover the non-stick pan is useful.

Remove the bones from the chicken thighs and pat the thighs dry.
(The bones can be used to make chicken stock.)

Heat 1 tablespoon of the vegetable oil with a pinch of salt over a medium-high heat in the non-stick pan. Add the chicken thighs, skin side down and opened out, and fry for 4–6 minutes until the skins are golden brown and crisp. Turn them over, reduce the heat to medium and leave them to continue cooking while you make the sauce. They will render a lot of fat, so it's a good idea to cover the pan with a splatter guard.

Meanwhile, peel and finely chop the ginger. Peel, halve and finely chop the onion. Lightly crush the cardamom pods to release the seeds.

Heat the remaining 2 tablespoons of the vegetable oil over a medium-high heat in the other pan. Add the cardamom pods and their seeds, the peppercorns and cumin seeds, and stir until the spices crackle. Add the onion with a pinch of salt and continue frying, stirring occasionally, until the onion is lightly browned.

Add the onion paste and stir it for 30 seconds. Add the ground coriander, chilli powder and turmeric, and continue stirring for a further 30 seconds to cook the spices. Watch closely so they do not burn.

Add the water and passata and continue stirring for about 1 minute to make a rich sauce. Stir in the bay leaf, fenugreek powder and garam masala. Season with salt and leave the gravy to simmer and thicken, uncovered. It will become darker when you add the fenugreek leaf powder. Stir in half the chopped ginger and leave to continue simmering while you chop enough coriander leaves to make about 4 tablespoons. Stir half the chopped coriander into the gravy.

Transfer the chicken thighs to the gravy, skin side up, cover the pan and leave them to simmer for 5 minutes, or until they are cooked through and tender. Adjust the seasoning with salt, if necessary. Sprinkle with the remaining chopped ginger and chopped coriander, and serve.

BENGALI CHICKEN KORMA

Bengal Murgh Korma

On weekends, when I take over kitchen duties from Mrs K, this is one of the recipes I turn to. It's fragrant and flavoursome and showcases the best of quick curries. This is a very light korma, without any almonds for thickening, so is a good recipe for anyone with a nut allergy, who normally can't enjoy kormas. Whisking the yogurt and cream with a little water helps prevent it splitting in the pan. If your gravy does split, however, you can bring it back by stirring in another tablespoon of yogurt or double cream. I suggest using Greek-style yogurt in all the recipes in this book because it has been strained, so it is less likely to split.

SERVES 4

600g chicken thigh fillets
250g Greek-style yogurt
2 tablespoons single cream
100ml water
fresh coriander leaves
1 tablespoon vegetable oil or ghee
1 dried bay leaf
2 tablespoons Onion Paste
  (page 218)
½ teaspoon red chilli powder, or
  to taste
½ teaspoon garam masala
¼ teaspoon ground turmeric
sea salt

For the tarka
4 green cardamom pods
1 teaspoon ghee
5cm piece of cinnamon stick
2 cloves
1 dried bay leaf

Assemble all the ingredients and equipment before you begin. You need a bowl, a whisk, a large sauté or frying pan and a small saucepan.

Cut the chicken thigh fillets into bite-sized pieces. Put the yogurt and cream in the bowl and whisk in 2 tablespoons of the water. Rinse and chop enough coriander leaves to make about 2 tablespoons.

Heat the vegetable oil over a medium-high heat in the sauté pan. Add the bay leaf and stir it around to flavour the oil. Add the onion paste and stir it into the oil for 30 seconds. Add the chicken pieces and continue stirring just until they are lightly coloured on all sides.

Stir in the remaining water, scraping the bottom of the pan. Add the chilli powder, garam masala and turmeric. Season with salt and stir for 30 seconds to cook the spices. Watch closely so they do not burn. Turn the heat to medium, whisk in the yogurt mixture and leave the chicken to simmer, stirring occasionally, for 10 minutes, or until it is cooked through and tender. Do not allow the mixture to boil, or the yogurt will split.

Just before serving, make the tarka. Lightly crush the cardamom pods to loosen the seeds. Melt the ghee in the saucepan over a high heat. Add the cardamom pods and seeds, the cinnamon stick, cloves and bay leaf, and stir until the spices crackle. Immediately pour this over the chicken mixture and stir in.

Adjust the seasoning with salt, if necessary, and stir in the chopped coriander just before serving.

ROYAL CHICKEN AND ALMOND CURRY

Nizami Badami Murg

This is a classic entertaining recipe that was once made for the royal courts of Hyderabad. The rich almonds-and-spice-infused gravy is also good to use with prawns, other seafood and vegetables. This is a liquid curry, so serve it with plenty of boiled basmati rice.

The secret to the sauce is how you blend your spices and how you make your onion paste. If you make your onion paste properly (page 218) – slowly cooking it until the onions' moisture evaporates and they brown – I don't think you will have any problems.

SERVES 4

250ml whole milk
a pinch of saffron threads
1 teaspoon vegetable oil
3 tablespoons Onion Paste
  (page 218)
½ cinnamon stick
1 dried bay leaf
2 teaspoons ground coriander
1 teaspoon ground cumin
¾ teaspoon garam masala, plus an
  extra pinch to garnish
½ teaspoon ground turmeric
250ml water
250g Greek-style yogurt
3 tablespoons ground almonds
10 ready-to-eat dried apricots
1 tablespoon raisins
600g chicken breast fillets
fresh coriander leaves
sea salt

For the spice powder

8 cloves
4 green cardamom pods
3 black cardamom pods
1 teaspoon black peppercorns
½ nutmeg

Assemble all the ingredients and equipment before you begin. You need a small saucepan, a non-stick pan for toasting the spices, a fine grater, a spice grinder, a large sauté or frying pan and a bowl.

Put the milk and saffron in the small saucepan over a medium-low heat and bring to a simmer. Turn off the heat and leave for the saffron to infuse the milk.

Next make the spice powder. Heat the dry non-stick pan over a high heat. Add the cloves, green and black cardamom pods and peppercorns. Finely grate in the nutmeg, then toast, stirring, until all the spices are aromatic. Tip the spices into the spice grinder and grind until a fine powder forms. Set aside.

Heat the vegetable oil over a medium-high heat in the sauté pan. Add the onion paste, cinnamon stick and bay leaf, and stir for 30 seconds. Add the spice powder, ground coriander, cumin, ½ teaspoon of the garam masala and the turmeric, and stir for a further 30 seconds to cook the spices. The paste will be very dark brown at this point. Add 125ml of the water, stirring until the mixture becomes smooth, then leave to simmer while you mix the yogurt.

Put the yogurt in the bowl with the remaining 125ml water and whisk well, then stir in the ground almonds.

Add the yogurt mixture to the pan, stirring to blend the ingredients. Add the saffron-infused milk and season with salt. Keep the heat low or the yogurt will split. Slice each of the dried apricots in half lengthways through the centre, adding the pieces to the gravy as you cut them. Add the raisins.

Cut the chicken fillets across the grain into strips about 1cm thick, then add them to the pan. Increase the heat to medium and leave the mixture to simmer gently, uncovered, for about 10 minutes until the chicken pieces are cooked through and tender.

Meanwhile, rinse and chop enough coriander leaves to make about 2 tablespoons.

When the chicken is tender, stir in the remaining garam masala and three-quarters of the chopped coriander. Adjust the seasoning with salt, if necessary. Sprinkle over the remaining chopped coriander and add a pinch of garam masala to serve.

GOAN CHICKEN CURRY

Galinha Kari

Goan food has a wonderful spicy heat to it – just think of vindaloos – and if there was a chilli rating on these recipes, I would definitely give this curry three chillies.

    I've given this recipe its kick by including four dried red chillies and ¼ teaspoon of black peppercorns in the spice powder. I'm OK to eat this with rice, but I know many people will be challenged – and I know my children won't be joining me. If you want to cut back on the fire, I suggest using only two dried red chillies and just five peppercorns. The heat will be less, but the flavour will still be beautiful.

SERVES 4

600g chicken thigh fillets
1 tablespoon vegetable oil
2½ tablespoons Onion Paste
   (page 218)
125ml water
3 tablespoons canned chopped
   tomatoes
1 teaspoon sugar
3 tablespoons Tamarind Liquid
   (page 223)
250ml coconut milk
sea salt
fresh coriander sprigs, to garnish

For the spice powder
5 green cardamom pods
4 large dried red chillies
4 teaspoons coriander seeds
2 teaspoons cumin seeds
¼ teaspoon black peppercorns

Assemble all the ingredients and equipment before you begin. You will need a spice grinder and a large sauté or frying pan with a lid.

First make the spice powder. Place the cardamom pods, chillies, coriander and cumin seeds and peppercorns into the spice grinder, and grind until a fine powder forms. Set aside.

Cut the chicken fillets into bite-sized pieces.

Heat the vegetable oil over a medium-high heat in the pan. Add the onion paste and stir it into the oil for 30 seconds. Tip in all the spice powder and stir for 30 seconds to cook the spices. Watch closely so they do not burn.

Lower the heat slightly, add the chicken pieces and stir until they are coated with the spices and onion mixture. Stir in the water, scraping the bottom of the pan. Season with salt and continue stirring for a further 4 minutes, or until the chicken pieces are coated in a thick brownish paste.

Add the tomatoes and sugar, stirring to break down any large tomato chunks. Stir in the tamarind liquid and coconut milk. Turn the heat down a little and leave the curry to simmer, covered, for 10 minutes, or until the chicken is cooked through and tender. Adjust the seasoning with salt, if necessary.

Meanwhile, rinse the coriander sprigs and then garnish the curry once served.

CHICKEN AND SPINACH CURRY

Murgh Palak Curry

My intention was to write a chicken and sorrel curry recipe, but as sorrel has such a short season it seemed more useful to give you a recipe using spinach. When you find bunches of sorrel on sale in the spring, however, grab several to use instead of spinach.

SERVES 4

600g chicken thigh fillets
200g baby spinach leaves, or sorrel
   leaves
3 long thin green chillies
2 tablespoons vegetable oil
1 tablespoon white poppy seeds
3 tablespoons Onion Paste (page
   218)
1 teaspoon Garlic Paste (page 220)
2 teaspoons ground coriander
1 teaspoon red chilli powder, or
   to taste
1 teaspoon garam masala
1 teaspoon ground cumin
200ml water
3 tablespoons Tamarind Liquid
   (page 223)
sea salt
fresh coriander sprigs, to garnish

Bring a large covered saucepan of water to the boil and assemble all the ingredients and other equipment before you begin. You also need a long-handled wooden spoon, a sieve or colander, a food processor fitted with a chopping blade, a non-stick pan for toasting the spices, a spice grinder and a large sauté or frying pan.

Cut the chicken thigh fillets into bite-sized pieces. Rinse the spinach leaves well. Remove the stalks from the green chillies, if necessary, then finely chop the chillies.

Drop the spinach leaves into the pan of boiling water, pressing them all down with a wooden spoon, then almost immediately drain them and rinse under cold running water to stop the cooking. Drain them again, squeezing out any excess water, then transfer them to the food processor. Add 1 tablespoon of the vegetable oil and blitz until puréed. Set aside.

Heat the dry non-stick pan over a high heat. Add the poppy seeds and stir until they are lightly browned, aromatic and pop. Transfer these to the spice grinder and finely grind. Set aside.

Heat the remaining 1 tablespoon of vegetable oil in the sauté pan over a medium-high heat. Add the green chillies and chicken. Season with a pinch of salt and stir to seal the chicken on all sides. Add the onion paste and garlic paste and stir them with the chicken for about 30 seconds. Add the ground coriander, chilli powder, garam masala and cumin. Season with salt and stir for 30 seconds to cook the spices. Watch closely so they do not burn.

Add the puréed spinach, stirring to blend the ingredients together. Stir in the poppy seed powder, then add the water and tamarind liquid and bring to the boil. Turn the heat down and leave the curry to simmer for 10 minutes, or until the chicken is cooked through and tender.

Meanwhile, rinse some coriander leaves for a garnish.

Adjust the seasoning with salt, if necessary. Garnish with coriander leaves and serve.

CHICKEN PERALEN

Keali Peralen

This is a classic curry from Kerala, and, in my opinion, just about every household makes this on the weekends – the way we have butter chicken in north India, they have chicken Peralen.

In Kerala, shallots are used more often than onions, and they are almost always fried and added just before serving for extra seasoning called a tarka, as in this recipe.

Coconut vinegar would also be used in Kerala, but I know that even when you find it in the UK it is very expensive, so ordinary white wine vinegar is just fine.

SERVES 4

600g chicken thigh fillets
1 onion
2 tablespoons coconut oil
10 fresh or dried curry leaves, plus extra fresh leaves, to garnish (optional)
2 tablespoons Onion Paste (page 218)
1 tablespoon white wine vinegar
125ml water
salt

For the spice powder
8 cloves
4 green cardamom pods
2 large dried red chillies
1 cinnamon stick
1 tablespoon coriander seeds
½ teaspoon fennel seeds
½ teaspoon ground turmeric
½ teaspoon black peppercorns

For the tarka
1 shallot
1 teaspoon coconut oil
½ teaspoon black mustard seeds
10 fresh curry leaves

Assemble all the ingredients and equipment before you begin. You will need a spice grinder, a large sauté or frying pan with a lid and a heavy-based saucepan.

First make the spice powder. Put the cloves, cardamom pods, dried chillies, cinnamon stick, coriander and fennel seeds, turmeric and peppercorns in the spice grinder, and grind until a fine powder forms.

Cut the chicken into bite-sized pieces and place in a large bowl. Stir in the spice powder and ¼ teaspoon of salt, making sure all the chicken pieces are coated. Set aside.

Halve, peel and thinly slice the onion.

Melt the coconut oil over a medium-high heat in the sauté pan. Add the onion with ½ teaspoon of salt and stir for 30 seconds so the onion starts softening. Add the curry leaves and the onion paste and stir the paste into the oil for 30 seconds.

Add the chicken pieces and stir to seal them and blend with the other ingredients, stirring constantly so the spices do not burn. Watch closely because they can burn quickly. Stir in the vinegar, which will evaporate almost immediately, then add the water, stirring and scraping the bottom of the pan until a thin paste forms.

Reduce the heat to medium, cover the pan and leave the curry to simmer for 10 minutes, stirring occasionally, or until the chicken is cooked through and tender.

Just before serving, make the tarka. Peel, halve and thinly slice the shallot. Melt the coconut oil over a medium-high heat in the saucepan. Add the mustard seeds and stir until they pop. Lower the heat, add the shallots and stir for a couple of seconds. Add the curry leaves and continue stirring until the shallots are lightly coloured.

When the chicken is tender, pour the tarka over and stir in. Adjust the seasoning with salt, if necessary. Garnish with a few fresh curry leaves if you have any, and serve.

PEPPER CHICKEN

Kozhi Varuval

This recipe is from Tamil Nadu, where they use peppers in every possible form – black pepper, fresh green chilli peppers, fresh red chilli peppers, dried red chilli peppers and red chilli powder. What I love about food from this part of the world is that cooks combine lots of hot spices like red chilli and black pepper, but they balance the flavours with cooling spices like cinnamon, fennel and star anise. It's very clever spicing.

SERVES 4

600g chicken thigh fillets
2 long thin green chillies
2 tablespoons coconut oil
20 fresh or dried curry leaves
2 tablespoons Onion Paste
  (page 218)
1 teaspoon Garlic Paste (page 220)
5 teaspoons Benares Curry Powder
  (page 223)
1 tablespoon ground coriander
½ teaspoon red chilli powder, or
  to taste
½ teaspoon ground turmeric
125ml water
sea salt
fresh coriander sprigs, to garnish

For the spice powder

2.5cm piece of cinnamon stick
1 clove
2 teaspoons black peppercorns
1 teaspoon cumin seeds
1 teaspoon fennel seeds

Assemble all the ingredients and equipment before you begin. You need a spice grinder and a large sauté or frying pan.

First make the spice powder. Put the cinnamon stick, clove, peppercorns and cumin and fennel seeds into the spice grinder, and grind until a fine powder forms. Set aside.

Cut the chicken thigh fillets into bite-sized pieces. Remove the stalk from the green chillies, if necessary, then cut the chillies in half lengthways.

Melt the coconut oil over a medium-high heat in the pan. Add the green chillies, curry leaves, onion paste and garlic paste, and stir the pastes into the oil for 30 seconds. Add the chicken pieces and stir them around for about 2 minutes until sealed on all sides.

Add the spice powder, Benares curry powder, ground coriander, chilli powder and turmeric. Season with salt and stir for 30 seconds to cook the spices. Watch closely so they do not burn. Add the water and continue stirring until a thick paste coats the chicken pieces.

Leave the chicken to simmer, uncovered, for a further 10–15 minutes, stirring occasionally, until the chicken is cooked through and tender, and most of the liquid in the gravy has evaporated.

Meanwhile, rinse the coriander sprigs to use for the garnish.

Adjust the seasoning with salt, if necessary, and serve garnished with coriander sprigs.

Atul's time-saving tip
I've improved on the preparation time for a traditional recipe by using onion paste, rather than having to chop lots of shallots, which you will find in most versions.

MALAY CHICKEN CURRY

Kari Ayam

When it comes to easy end-of-the-day cooking, this is a straightforward one-pot meal. It doesn't need anything extra, but you can serve it with boiled rice or naan if you like. I've used chicken thigh fillets in this, but you can also use boneless chicken breasts. If you have drumsticks in the fridge, by all means use them, but the recipe will take longer than thirty minutes to complete because of the bones.

SERVES 4

9 well-scrubbed new potatoes (see Atul's tip, page 29)
600g chicken thigh fillets
3 garlic cloves
1 banana shallot, or 2 ordinary shallots
1 tablespoon vegetable oil
½ cinnamon stick
1 star anise
2 tablespoons Onion Paste (page 218)
1 teaspoon Garlic Paste (page 220)
10 fresh or dried curry leaves, plus extra fresh leaves to garnish (optional)
1 teaspoon ground turmeric
125ml coconut milk
300ml water
2 tablespoons Tamarind Liquid (page 223)
2cm piece of fresh ginger
sea salt

For the spice powder
1 large dried red chilli
½ cinnamon stick
1 star anise
1 tablespoon coriander seeds
1 teaspoon cumin seeds
1 teaspoon fennel seeds

Bring a covered saucepan of salted water to the boil and assemble all the ingredients and other equipment before you begin. You also need a non-stick pan to toast the spices in, a spice grinder, a large sauté or frying pan and a sieve or colander.

Get the potatoes cooking as quickly as possible. Quarter the potatoes lengthways, adding them to the boiling water as you cut. Be careful the water doesn't splash you as you add the potatoes. Re-cover the pan and return the water to the boil, then boil, uncovered, for 15 minutes, or until the potatoes are tender. When the potatoes are tender, drain them well, return to the pan, cover to keep hot and set aside.

Meanwhile, make the spice powder. Heat the dry non-stick pan over a high heat. Add the dried chilli, cinnamon stick, star anise and coriander, cumin and fennel seeds, and stir until they are aromatic. Tip the spices into the spice grinder and grind until a fine powder forms.

Cut the chicken thigh fillets into bite-sized pieces. Peel and thinly slice the garlic cloves. Peel, halve and thinly slice the shallot.

Heat the vegetable oil over a medium-high heat in the pan. Add the garlic, cinnamon and star anise, and stir them around to flavour the oil. Add the shallot and continue stirring until it is lightly coloured. Add the onion paste and garlic paste, and stir them into the shallot for 30 seconds. Add the spice powder, curry leaves and turmeric, and continue stirring for 30 seconds to cook the turmeric. Watch closely so the spices do not burn.

Add the coconut milk, water and tamarind liquid. Season with salt and stir to make sure nothing is sticking to the bottom of the pan. Bring to the boil, stirring, then reduce the heat to medium. Stir in the chicken and leave the curry to gently simmer for 10 minutes, or until the chicken is cooked through and tender.

Meanwhile, peel and very finely chop the ginger.

When the chicken is cooked, stir the ginger into the pan with the potatoes. Adjust the seasoning with salt, if necessary, and garnish with fresh curry leaves, if you have any.

CALCUTTA CHICKEN CURRY

Kolkata Murgi Kori

This is a thirty-minute Sunday affair. Just as we in the UK have a roast lunch on Sundays, in Kolkata it's lamb or chicken that's cooked, and it's a big ceremony. If I was making a full-blown Bengali Sunday lunch it would take more than an hour, so I have taken a few shortcuts here by using onion paste and boiling the potatoes separately, but I think I have still delivered. If you have time, however, cook the potatoes with the chicken and there will be even more flavour. The final result is something I can't describe in words, because it's just a flavour transformation that happens in the pan.

Growing up in a Punjabi household in east India was great fun, not least of all because we were constantly mixing flavours in our food. There was so much learning going on in the kitchen, and I adored that part of my upbringing. Today, I still just love the smell of the turmeric and chilli powder cooking, especially with the moisture from the potatoes. There is so much 'drama' going on in the pan at that point and it looks lovely. My Bengali friends are going to be salivating when I post a photo of this on Instagram.

SERVES 4

9 well-scrubbed new potatoes (see Atul's tip, page 29)
mustard oil
2 dried bay leaves
1½ teaspoons ground turmeric
1 teaspoon red chilli powder, or to taste
650ml water, plus extra, as needed
600g chicken breast fillets
4 green cardamom pods
2 long thin green chillies
1½ tomatoes
10 black peppercorns
1 cinnamon stick
3 tablespoons Onion Paste (page 218)
2¼ teaspoons garam masala
fresh coriander leaves
sea salt

Assemble all the ingredients and equipment before you begin. You need 2 large sauté or frying pans, both with lids.

Quarter the potatoes lengthways to make long wedges. Heat about 1 tablespoon of the mustard oil over a medium-high heat in one of the pans. Add the potatoes and 1 bay leaf, stirring to coat the potatoes in oil. Add 1 teaspoon of the turmeric, the chilli powder and plenty of salt, and stir for 30 seconds to cook the spices. Watch closely so they do not burn.

Pour in 400ml of the water, season with salt and bring to the boil. Cover the pan and gently boil the potatoes over a medium-high heat for 10 minutes until they are almost tender.

Meanwhile, cut the chicken fillets into bite-sized pieces. Lightly crush the cardamom pods to release the seeds. Remove the stalks from the green chillies, if necessary, then halve the chillies lengthways. Cut the tomatoes into wedges.

Heat 2 tablespoons of the mustard oil over a medium-high heat in the other pan. Add the cardamom pods and their seeds, the peppercorns, the remaining bay leaf and the cinnamon stick, and stir until the spices crackle. Watch closely so nothing burns. Add the onion paste and stir it into the oil for 30 seconds.

continued on page 174

Add the chicken and green chillies and stir to seal the chicken on all sides. Stir in the remaining ½ teaspoon turmeric and 1 teaspoon of the garam masala. Season with salt and stir for 30 seconds to cook the spices. Add 125ml of the water to prevent the chicken from catching on the bottom of the pan.

Stir in the tomatoes, cover the pan and leave the chicken to gently simmer for 5 minutes, stirring occasionally. You want the tomatoes to soften and start giving off their juice, but still hold their shape.

When the potatoes are almost tender, add them and all their cooking liquid into the pan with the chicken. Add the remaining 125ml water plus extra, if necessary, so the potatoes and chicken pieces are almost covered. Cover the pan and leave the curry to gently boil over a medium heat for 5 minutes, or until the chicken is cooked through and tender and the potatoes are tender.

Meanwhile, rinse and finely chop enough coriander leaves to make about 4 tablespoons, reserving a few whole leaves for garnishing.

Stir the chopped coriander and remaining 1¼ teaspoons garam masala into the curry. Adjust the seasoning with salt, if necessary, and garnish with the coriander leaves.

GOLDEN GARLIC CHICKEN THIGHS

Kadak Murgi

Supermarkets don't usually sell boneless chicken thighs with the skin on, so you have to go to a butcher for these thighs. If, however, you want to make this with bone-in chicken thighs, allow about 20 minutes for them to cook under the grill.

SERVES 4

1 tablespoon Garlic Paste (page 220)
2 teaspoons garam masala
½ teaspoon ground turmeric
4 boned chicken thighs, skin on
vegetable oil for brushing the grill rack
sea salt

Preheat the grill to high, line a grill pan with kitchen foil and assemble all the ingredients before you begin. You also need a bowl.

Mix the garlic paste, garam masala and turmeric together in the bowl. Add the chicken thighs and stir until they are well coated.

Brush the grill rack with oil. Place the thighs on the rack, skin side up, and opened out flat. Sprinkle with salt.

Place the grill rack under the grill and grill for 8 minutes, or until well browned. Turn over and grill for a further 6–8 minutes until the chicken is cooked through and tender.

DUCK 'ROAST' CURRY WITH ROAST POTATOES

Tarav Roast Kari

SERVES 4

4 duck breasts
1 heaped tablespoon Ginger-Garlic
  Paste (page 220)
1 tablespoon white wine vinegar
4 tablespoons coconut oil
about 250ml water
6 shallots
3 green cardamom pods
2 cloves
2.5cm piece of cinnamon stick
250ml coconut milk
fresh coriander sprigs
salt and freshly ground black pepper

For the roast potatoes

12 new potatoes (see Atul's tip,
  page 29)
2 tablespoons coconut oil
small handful of fresh or dried
  curry leaves

For the spice powder

8 cloves
4 green cardamom pods
5cm piece of cinnamon stick
2 tablespoons ground coriander
1 teaspoon red chilli powder, or
  to taste
½ teaspoon ground fennel
½ teaspoon ground black pepper
½ teaspoon ground turmeric
¼ teaspoon ground cumin

Preheat the oven to 220°C/Fan 200°C/Gas Mark 7, bring a large covered saucepan of salted water to the boil and assemble all the ingredients and other equipment before you begin. You also need a roasting tray, a bowl, a spice grinder and a large sauté or frying pan.

I call this a 'roast', but roasting actually has nothing to do with cooking the duck. This is typical of recipes from Kerala, where anything that is pan-fried is called 'roasted'. I think this might be a hangover from the days when the English or Portuguese had roast meals, so the locals decided they would have a 'roast' curry with roast potatoes cooked over a charcoal fire.

I decided I wanted to create a whole meal – a Sunday lunch with an Indian twist, you could say – so I've included roast potatoes. They might take your total cooking time over the thirty-minute limit if you aren't completely organised before you start cooking, so if you are in a hurry you can just leave them out.

In Kerala, this dish would most likely be made with duck legs, but they don't cook quickly enough to be included in a thirty-minute recipe. If you don't have any shallots, use a couple of tablespoons of Onion Paste (page 218) instead.

Get the potatoes cooking as quickly as possible. Halve the potatoes, adding them to the boiling water as you cut. Be careful that the water doesn't splash you. Re-cover the pan and return the water to the boil, then boil, uncovered, for 15 minutes, or until the potatoes are almost tender.

Add the roasting tray to the oven to heat up after the potatoes have boiled for 12 minutes.

Meanwhile, skin the duck breasts and cut them into bite-sized pieces. Set aside in the bowl.

Make the spice powder. Put the cloves, cardamom pods, cinnamon, ground coriander, chilli powder, ground fennel, black pepper, turmeric and ground cumin in the spice grinder, and grind until a fine powder forms.

Tip the spice powder into the bowl with the duck, season with salt and stir so all the duck pieces are well coated. Add the ginger-garlic paste and vinegar and stir again to blend the ingredients.

Melt 2 tablespoons of the coconut oil over a medium heat in the sauté pan. Add the duck pieces and stir for about 30 seconds to sear and cook the spice powder. The oil will be absorbed, so watch closely so the spices

continued on page 178

don't burn. Pour in enough water to just cover the meat, stir and then leave to simmer, uncovered.

Drain the potatoes well, shaking off as much water as possible, then transfer them to the roasting tray. Add the 2 tablespoons of coconut oil and the curry leaves, season with salt and pepper and toss together. Place the tray in the oven and roast the potatoes for 15 minutes, stirring occasionally, or until the potatoes are tender and browned.

When the potatoes go into the oven, strain the duck pieces and set aside the duck and cooking liquid separately. Wipe out the sauté pan. Peel, halve and slice the shallots. Crush the cardamom pods to loosen the seeds.

Return the wiped pan to a medium-high heat. Melt the remaining 2 tablespoons of coconut oil in the pan. Add the cardamom pods and their seeds, the cloves and cinnamon, and stir until the spices crackle. Add the shallots and stir until they are lightly coloured.

Turn the heat to high and slowly stir in the reserved duck cooking juices – stand back because it will generate a great deal of steam. Stir in the coconut milk. This is like adding cream towards the end of cooking in a western recipe, and will mellow the flavour, as well as enrich and thicken the gravy. Adjust the seasoning with salt, if necessary.

Reduce the heat and stir in the duck pieces. Leave the curry to simmer, uncovered and stirring occasionally, until the potatoes are ready to come out of the oven.

Meanwhile, rinse a few coriander sprigs to use for garnishing.

I've eaten similar dishes to this in Keralan homes many times and they are served with the potatoes around the edge of a serving platter and the curry in the centre. Add a few coriander sprigs for garnish.

CURRIED DUCK BREASTS

Masaledar Bathak

This is such a versatile recipe – you can dress it up for a quick dinner party dish by making the spiced spinach from the sea bass recipe on page 122, or serve it for a simple family supper with reheated leftover cooked potatoes. If you have time, the initial frying that renders the fat can be done in the morning, then the duck breasts can be left to cool completely, covered and chilled until 15 minutes before they go in the oven for the final roasting.

I like my duck breasts medium rare, but if you want them medium, cook them for an extra 3 minutes.

SERVES 4

4 boneless duck breasts, skin on
1½ tablespoons Benares Curry
    Powder (page 223)
sea salt

Preheat the oven to 200°C/Fan 180°C/Gas Mark 6 and assemble all the ingredients and equipment before you begin. You need an ovenproof sauté or frying pan large enough to hold the duck breasts in a single layer.

Use a small, sharp knife to cut a diamond pattern in the skin side of each duck breast, cutting through the skin and fat, but not into the flesh.

Heat the pan over a high heat. Add the duck breasts, skin side down, and fry for 5 minutes, or until the skin is browned and crisp and the fat has been rendered out. Use a large spoon to remove the fat from the pan as it accumulates.

Turn the duck breasts skin side up. Divide the curry powder among the breasts and use the back of a wooden spoon to rub it into the cuts. Sprinkle with salt.

Transfer to the oven and roast for 4 minutes for medium rare, or until they feel soft when pressed. Cover with foil and leave to rest for 5 minutes, before slicing.

COUNTRY GUINEA FOWL CURRY

Desi Kukkar Curry

SERVES 4

1 guinea fowl, weighing about 1.2kg, skinned, cut into portions, boned and breasts halved widthways
1½ onions
2 long thin green chillies
1 black cardamom pod
1 green cardamom pod
2 tablespoons vegetable oil
1 teaspoon cumin seeds
2 tomatoes
fresh coriander leaves
1 tablespoon ground coriander
1 teaspoon ground turmeric
¼ teaspoon red chilli powder, or to taste
½ teaspoon garam masala
2 tablespoons Ginger-Garlic Paste (page 220)
300ml water
sea salt

For the spice paste
½ lemon
2 tablespoons vegetable oil
2¼ teaspoons ground coriander
1¼ teaspoons dried fenugreek leaf powder
1¼ teaspoons garam masala
1 teaspoon red chilli powder, or to taste
1½ teaspoons Ginger-Garlic Paste (page 220)

Preheat the oven to 200°C/Fan 180°C/Gas Mark 6, line a baking tray with kitchen foil, shiny side up, and assemble all the ingredients and other equipment before you begin. You also need a large non-reactive bowl and a large sauté or frying pan with a lid.

If your household is anything like mine, guinea fowl isn't an everyday supper dish. I like it so much, however, that I just had to include a recipe for it in this book, so here's one that you might consider more suitable for supper with friends than a mid-week family meal in a hurry. The bird does have to be boned to cook within thirty minutes, so I suggest you buy it from a butcher and get him or her to do all the work for you. Ask for the bones and add them to the gravy mixture when you add the water. They really do add extra flavour.

Personally, I love country-style cooking from the Punjab. It's so me. The tomatoes break down slightly to thicken the rich gravy, and the dish maintains its rustic nature.

First make the spice paste. Squeeze 2 tablespoons of lemon juice into the bowl. Stir in the vegetable oil, ground coriander, fenugreek powder, garam masala, chilli powder and the ginger-garlic paste. Season with salt.

Add the guinea fowl pieces to the spice paste and mix together until they are coated all over. Transfer the guinea fowl pieces to the roasting tray in a single layer and roast for 18–20 minutes, turning the pieces over after 10 minutes, until cooked through and the juices run clear.

Meanwhile, peel, quarter and slice the onions. Remove the stalks from the green chillies, if necessary, then slice the chillies. Lightly crush both the black and green cardamom pods to loosen the seeds.

Heat the vegetable oil over a medium-high heat in the pan. Add the black and green cardamom pods and their seeds and the cumin seeds, and stir until the cumin seeds crackle. Add the onions and chillies with a pinch of salt. Cover the pan and leave the onions to cook for 5–8 minutes, stirring occasionally, until they are lightly coloured. Adding the salt helps the onions to cook quicker and covering the pan retains the moisture from the onions.

While the onions are cooking, coarsely chop the tomatoes. Rinse and chop enough coriander leaves to make about 2 tablespoons.

Add the tomatoes, ground coriander, turmeric, chilli powder, garam masala and ginger-garlic paste to the pan, and stir for 30 seconds to cook the spices. Watch closely so they do not burn. Add the water and bring to the boil, stirring. Reduce the heat to medium-low, use the back of a spoon to break up the tomatoes, cover the pan and leave to simmer until the guinea fowl finishes roasting.

When the guinea fowl is cooked through, transfer it and all the cooking juices that have accumulated in the tray to the pan with the tomato gravy and stir together. Adjust the seasoning with salt, if necessary. Sprinkle with the chopped coriander and serve.

Atul's time-saving tips
For a quicker, more everyday version of this recipe, simmer bite-sized pieces of chicken thigh fillets and boneless chicken breasts in the gravy.

You can also make the spice paste early in the day and leave the guinea fowl (or chicken pieces) to marinate so all you have to do is roast the pieces and make the gravy just before serving.

MEAT

HYDERABADI LAMB CURRY

Mahi Gosht

This is quite an amazing curry that I was introduced to by a blog I occasionally read, *Ruchik Randhap: Food and Memories of Mangalore*. The curry's sweet, salty, sour and spicy – and I'd never cooked anything quite like this before I started developing my version. I'm happy that I'm including it in this collection. The gravy has a lot of character and texture, but if you wanted to make it into a thin curry stir in 250ml extra water. It will still have a good texture.

SERVES 4

600g boneless lamb rump or neck fillet
15g piece of jaggery or palm sugar
2 tablespoons vegetable oil
1 tablespoon ground coriander
1 teaspoon red chilli powder, or to taste
1 teaspoon ground turmeric
4 tablespoons Onion Paste (page 218)
1 teaspoon Garlic Paste (page 220)
250ml water
fresh coriander leaves
4 tablespoons Tamarind Liquid (page 223)
sea salt

For the nut and spice powder

4 tablespoons desiccated coconut
2 tablespoons sesame seeds
1½ tablespoons blanched raw unsalted peanuts
1 tablespoon coriander seeds
1 tablespoon white poppy seeds
½ teaspoon cumin seeds

Assemble all the ingredients and equipment before you begin. You need a non-stick pan for toasting the spices, a spice grinder and a large non-stick sauté or frying pan with a lid.

First make the nut and spice powder. Heat the dry non-stick pan over a low heat. Add the coconut, sesame seeds, peanuts and coriander, poppy and cumin seeds, and stir until the spices are aromatic and the coconut is lightly browned. Watch closely so nothing burns. Tip the mixture into the spice grinder and grind until a coarse powder forms. Set aside.

Cut the lamb into bite-sized pieces, trimming and discarding any fat. Coarsely chop the palm sugar.

Heat the vegetable oil over a high heat in the sauté pan. Add the lamb and stir for about 2 minutes until it is browned on all sides. Lower the heat to medium-high, add the ground coriander, chilli powder and turmeric, and stir for 30 seconds to cook the spices. Watch closely so they do not burn. Add the onion paste and garlic paste and continue stirring for a further 30 seconds.

Stir in the water, season with salt and bring to the boil. Reduce the heat to low, cover the pan and leave the lamb to simmer for 7 minutes, or until the lamb is almost tender.

Meanwhile, rinse and chop enough coriander leaves to make about 2 tablespoons.

Stir the spice powder, palm sugar and tamarind liquid into the gravy, stirring to dissolve the palm sugar. The gravy will become thicker when you add the spice powder, because of the coconut it contains. Leave to bubble, uncovered, for a further 3–5 minutes until the lamb is tender.

Adjust the seasoning with salt, if necessary, and sprinkle with the chopped coriander to serve.

LAMB WITH GREEN CHILLIES

Katchi Mirch Gosht

This rich dish has a wonderful flavour with just a hint of heat. With an eye on the clock I suggest marinating the lamb for 5 minutes, but if you have time you can leave it overnight.

If you can't find black cardamom pods or black cumin seeds, don't worry and just replace them with the conventional green pods and tan-coloured seeds. It can also be difficult to find ground fennel, so I toast and grind my own (page 227), but if you find it, by all means buy it.

SERVES 4

600g boneless lamb rump or
  neck fillet
225g Greek-style yogurt
2.5cm piece of fresh ginger
2 long thin green chillies
4 green cardamom pods
1 black cardamom pod
1 tablespoon vegetable oil
1 blade of mace
4cm piece of cinnamon stick
2 tablespoons Onion Paste
  (page 218)
2½ tablespoons Benares Curry
  Powder (page 223)
200ml water
a pinch of saffron threads
fresh coriander leaves
125ml double cream
2 teaspoons ground fennel
sea salt

For the spice powder
4 teaspoons coriander seeds
2 teaspoons cumin seeds
1 teaspoon black cumin seeds
¼ teaspoon black peppercorns

Assemble all the ingredients and equipment before you begin. You need a non-stick pan for toasting the spices, a spice grinder, a large non-reactive bowl, a large non-stick sauté or frying pan with a lid and a small heatproof bowl.

First make the spice powder. Heat the dry non-stick pan over a high heat. Add the coriander seeds, ordinary and black cumin seeds and peppercorns, and stir until they are aromatic. Tip the spices into the spice grinder and grind until a fine powder forms. Set aside.

Cut the lamb into bite-sized pieces, trimming and discarding any fat. Put the lamb, spice powder and yogurt the large bowl. Season with salt and mix together so all the lamb pieces are coated. Set aside for 5 minutes to marinate.

Meanwhile, peel and thinly slice the ginger. Remove the stalks from the green chillies, if necessary, then de-seed and finely chop the chillies. Lightly crush the green and black cardamom pods to loosen the seeds.

Heat the vegetable oil over a medium-high heat in the sauté pan. Add the ginger, green chillies, green and black cardamom pods with the seeds, the mace and cinnamon stick, and stir until the cardamom pods crackle. Add the onion paste and curry powder and stir them into the oil for 30 seconds, then add the water and bring to the boil, stirring.

Stir in the lamb and all the marinade. Cover the pan and bring the mixture to the boil. Boil for about 2 minutes, then reduce the heat to low and leave to simmer for 8–10 minutes until the lamb is tender.

Meanwhile, bring a kettle of water to the boil. Put the saffron in the small bowl, add 2 teaspoons of boiling water and set aside. Rinse and chop enough coriander leaves to make about 2 tablespoons.

When the lamb is tender, uncover the pan, turn the heat to high and return the curry to the boil. Stir in the cream, saffron and ground fennel, and leave to boil for a further 2 minutes. Adjust the seasoning with salt, if necessary, and sprinkle with the chopped coriander to serve.

LAMB WITH OKRA

Bhindi Gosht

I was so pleased when I was able to write this recipe so it could be completed within the thirty-minute limit. The key is simply to have the oven preheated to the correct temperature before you start cooking, then you should have plenty of time to roast the lamb even if your preference is well done. I serve this Punjabi recipe with naan breads or rotis.

If you can't find fresh okra, use frozen, straight from the freezer. And although okra is one of my favourite vegetables, I realise it isn't to everyone's taste, so substitute green beans if you'd rather.

SERVES 4

600g boneless lamb rump or neck fillets, at room temperature
200g okra
2 mild green chillies
2 red onions
2.5cm piece of fresh ginger
2 tablespoons vegetable oil
2 teaspoons cumin seeds
4 teaspoons ground coriander
1½ teaspoons garam masala
1 teaspoon red chilli powder, or to taste
1 teaspoon ground turmeric
1 teaspoon dried fenugreek leaf powder
1 spring onion
fresh coriander leaves
sea salt

For the spice paste
½ lemon
1 tablespoon Garlic Paste (page 220)
1 tablespoon vegetable oil
2 teaspoons dried fenugreek leaf powder
2 teaspoons ground coriander
½ teaspoon red chilli powder, or to taste
½ teaspoon garam masala

Remove the lamb from the fridge so it comes to room temperature. Preheat the oven to 200°C/Fan 180°C/Gas Mark 6, line a roasting tray with kitchen foil, shiny side up, and assemble all the ingredients and other equipment before you begin. You also need a large non-reactive bowl and a large non-stick sauté or frying pan with a lid.

Cut the lamb into bite-sized pieces, trimming and discarding any fat, then put it in the bowl. To make the paste, squeeze in 2 tablespoons of lemon juice, then add the garlic paste, vegetable oil, dried fenugreek leaf powder, ground coriander, chilli powder and garam masala, and season with salt. Mix everything together so the lamb is well coated.

Spread out the lamb in a single layer in the roasting tray and roast for 20 minutes, or until tender. It should be medium-well at this point, but you can roast for longer or less time, depending on how you like your lamb cooked.

Meanwhile, remove the stalk ends from the okra, then slice the pods lengthways and cut into bite-sized pieces.

Remove the stalks from the green chillies, if necessary, but leave the chillies whole. Peel, halve and thinly slice the onions. Peel and roughly chop the ginger.

Heat 2 tablespoons of the vegetable oil over a medium-high heat in the pan. Add the cumin seeds and stir until they crackle. Add the chopped ginger, ground coriander, garam masala, chilli powder, turmeric and fenugreek leaf powder, and continue stirring for 30 seconds to cook the spices. Watch closely so they do not burn.

Add the okra, onions and green chillies to the pan. Season with salt and continue stirring until the onion is softened, but not coloured.

Cover the pan, reduce the heat to medium-low and leave the vegetables to steam-cook with just the liquid that comes out of the okra and onions for a further 2 minutes, or until the okra is tender, but still holding its shape.

continued on page 190

While the okra finishes cooking, trim and finely chop the spring onion. Rinse and chop enough coriander leaves to make about 1 tablespoon. Set both aside.

When the lamb is tender and cooked to your liking, transfer it and all the cooking juices that have accumulated in the tray to the pan with the okra, stirring to blend. Adjust the seasoning with salt, if necessary, and sprinkle with the spring onion and chopped coriander just before serving.

Atul's time-saving tip

If you want to get ahead, rub the lamb pieces with the spice paste in the morning, cover and leave in the fridge all day, ready for cooking in the evening. Just remember to remove the meat from the fridge when you start preheating the oven, so it returns to room temperature before cooking.

LAMB SLOPPY JOES

Keema Pau

Here's an example of street food from Mumbai at its best. The city is the most cosmopolitan in India, and its cooking has absorbed the influences of the Parsees, the British and the Portuguese – they have all left their mark. I haven't been able to pin down exactly which culture gave *keema paus* to Mumbai, but I suspect the Portuguese or British. As a younger person, I loved this because it was heavily laced with spices and butter, but, alas, as time goes by I shy away from it. I just don't enjoy that heavy food anymore, and tend to make my own version with less fat. This version does include added butter for richness, but not as much as I would have once used.

  Pau is the generic Hindi word for 'bread'. You might be able to buy individual buns called *paus* at an Indian food shop, but otherwise soft hamburger buns are ideal. You can also replace the lamb mince with beef mince, if you like.

MAKES 4

3cm piece of fresh ginger
4 green cardamom pods
1 black cardamom pod
2 garlic cloves
1½ red onions
2 tablespoons vegetable oil
1 dried bay leaf
1 star anise
4cm piece of cinnamon stick
1 tablespoon Onion Paste
  (page 218)
300g lamb mince
2 teaspoons ground coriander
2 teaspoons ground cumin
2 teaspoons garam masala
½ teaspoon ground turmeric
8 tablespoons canned chopped
  tomatoes
fresh coriander sprigs
½ lemon
a large knob of butter, about 15g,
  plus extra for buttering the buns
4 *paus* or soft hamburger buns,
  to serve
1 tomato, to serve
olive oil
sea salt

Remove the butter from the fridge for it to become spreadable and assemble all the ingredients and equipment before you begin. You need 2 large sauté or frying pans, both of which are non-stick.

Peel and finely chop the ginger. Lightly crush the green and black cardamom pods to release the seeds. Peel and thinly slice the garlic cloves. Peel, halve and thinly slice the onions and set aside the slices from half an onion for serving.

Heat the vegetable oil over a medium-high heat in one of the sauté pans. Add the cardamom pods and the seeds, the bay leaf, star anise and the cinnamon stick, and stir for 30 seconds to flavour the oil. Add the onion paste and stir it into the oil for 30 seconds. Add the slices from one onion, the ginger, garlic and a pinch of salt, and continue stirring, until the onion is softened, but not coloured.

Add the lamb mince to the pan, turn up the heat and stir continuously for about 5 minutes to break up the meat and brown it. It should be virtually cooked at this point.

Reduce the heat to low, stir in the ground coriander, cumin, garam masala and the turmeric, and stir for 30 seconds to cook the spices. Watch closely so they do not burn. Stir in the canned tomatoes and leave the mixture to simmer, stirring occasionally. Watch closely so the meat doesn't burn on the bottom of the pan, but you do want it to brown nicely. If the mince does catch on the bottom of the pan, however, stir in a little water to release the crusty bits, which will add flavour. You just want to make sure you're not stirring in any burnt bits.

continued on page 193

Meanwhile, rinse the coriander sprigs. Set 4 aside for garnishing and chop enough leaves to make about 2 tablespoons. Squeeze 1 tablespoon of juice from the lemon half.

Stir three-quarters of the chopped coriander and all the lemon juice into the lamb, then add the butter and stir as it melts. Adjust the seasoning with salt, if necessary, and leave the mixture to continue simmering while you fry the buns.

Open the *paus* or hamburger buns. Heat about 1 teaspoon of the olive oil in the other pan. Lightly butter the split sides of each bun. Put 1 or 2 split buns in the pan and toast on the buttered sides. Toast the remaining breads, adding a little extra oil to the pan, as necessary.

Thinly slice the tomato. Mix the reserved onion and tomato slices together to make a salad for serving, just like street vendors in Mumbai do.

Place the opened buns on plates and divide the lamb mixture among them. Top with the onion and tomato salad and garnish each with a coriander leaf.

LAMB WITH CARDAMOM AND YOGURT

Lamb Dhaniwal Korma

This is a favourite recipe of mine. Cardamom is the important flavour here, so make sure you have a fresh supply of green cardamom pods or ground cardamom before cooking. Naans or pilau rice is the ideal accompaniment to serve with this.

SERVES 4

600g boneless lamb rump
  or neck fillet
2.5cm piece of fresh ginger
6 green cardamom pods
3 garlic cloves
1½ tablespoons vegetable oil
4 cloves
3 tablespoons Onion Paste
  (page 218)
1 tablespoon ground coriander
1 teaspoon red chilli powder, or
  to taste
1 teaspoon garam masala
1 teaspoon ground turmeric
¼ teaspoon ground black pepper
250ml water, plus an extra
  2 teaspoons
small pinch of saffron threads
2 tablespoons Greek-style yogurt
fresh coriander leaves
½ lemon
sea salt

Assemble all the ingredients and equipment before you begin. You need a large heavy-based, non-stick saucepan with a lid.

Cut the lamb into bite-sized pieces, trimming and discarding any fat. Peel and finely chop the ginger. Lightly crush the cardamom pods to release the seeds. Peel and thinly slice the garlic cloves.

Heat the vegetable oil over a medium-high heat in the saucepan. Add the cardamom pods with the seeds and the cloves and stir until they crackle. Add the ginger and garlic and stir to flavour the oil, making sure the garlic doesn't over-brown.

Add the onion paste and continue stirring for 30 seconds until it begins to 'loosen', again watching closely so it doesn't burn. Turn the heat to very low and stir in the ground coriander, chilli powder, garam masala, turmeric and black pepper, and continue stirring for 30 seconds–1 minute to cook the spices.

Stir in the lamb, increase the heat to high and stir until it is browned on all sides and coated in the spice mixture. It's important to watch closely so nothing burns at this point. Stir in 250ml of the water and the saffron. Season with salt and bring to the boil, stirring.

Reduce the heat, cover the pan and leave the lamb to simmer for 10 minutes, or until it is tender. Top up the liquid, if necessary, so the lamb is always submerged.

Meanwhile, mix the yogurt and remaining 2 teaspoons of water together. Rinse and finely chop enough coriander leaves to make about 2 tablespoons. Squeeze 2 teaspoons of lemon juice.

When the lamb is tender, stir the yogurt mixture into the pan. Add the lemon juice and adjust the seasoning with salt, if necessary, then stir in the chopped coriander to serve.

WHITE LAMB CURRY

Safed Gosht

This is a classic white curry from Gujarat. It isn't, however, 'white', just a much paler colour than most lamb curries. Take great care when you are toasting the cashews, coconut and spices to only very lightly colour them, or the finished dish will be darker than desired.

SERVES 4

600g boneless lamb rump or
    neck fillet
1 tablespoon vegetable oil
4 tablespoons Onion Paste
    (page 218)
fresh coriander sprigs
125ml water
1 teaspoon garam masala
sea salt

For the cashew and spice paste
60g raw unsalted cashew nuts
2 tablespoons desiccated coconut
1 tablespoon white poppy seeds
1 tablespoon sesame seeds
250ml water
4 tablespoons Greek-style yogurt

Assemble all the ingredients and equipment before you begin. You need a large non-stick sauté or frying pan with a lid, a non-stick pan for toasting the nuts, coconut and spices, a large bowl and a spice grinder.

Cut the lamb into bite-sized pieces, discarding any fat.

Heat the vegetable oil over a medium-high heat in the sauté pan. Stir the onion paste into the oil for 30 seconds. Add the lamb, increase the heat to high and stir to brown on all sides. Lower the heat and leave to continue cooking, stirring occasionally, while you make the paste. Watch carefully so the lamb doesn't catch on the bottom of the pan.

Meanwhile, to start the cashew and spice paste, heat the other dry non-stick pan over a low heat. Add the cashew nuts to the pan and stir until they are toasted, but not coloured, then immediately tip them into the bowl. Add the coconut to the pan and stir until toasted, but only very lightly coloured, then add it to the cashews. Turn the heat to high, add the poppy and sesame seeds to the pan and stir until they pop. Tip all these ingredients into the spice grinder and grind until a fine powder forms.

Tip the powder into the bowl. Whisk in 250ml of the water and the yogurt. Stir this mixture into the pan with the lamb, cover and leave to simmer for 5 minutes.

Meanwhile, rinse and chop enough coriander leaves and stalks to make about 2 tablespoons.

Stir 125ml of water and the garam masala into the lamb, re-cover the pan and leave the curry to simmer for a further 5 minutes, or until the lamb is tender. Adjust the seasoning with salt, if necessary, and sprinkle with the chopped coriander to serve.

LAMB CURRY

Kurimari Ghassi

This is a fabulous lamb curry and on my visits to Bangalore I never fail to try this authentic recipe from the region.

SERVES 4

600g boneless lamb rump or
   neck fillet
1.5cm piece of fresh ginger
1 tablespoon coconut oil
2 heaped tablespoons Onion Paste
   (page 218)
250ml water
½ lime
fresh coriander sprigs
sea salt

For the spice powder

5 tablespoons desiccated coconut
2 large dried red chillies
2 cloves
1 cinnamon stick
1 tablespoon coriander seeds
1 tablespoon white poppy seeds
1 teaspoon cumin seeds

Assemble all the ingredients and equipment before you begin. You need a non-stick pan for toasting the coconut and spices, a spice grinder and a large non-stick sauté or frying pan with a lid.

First make the spice powder. Heat the dry non-stick pan over a low heat. Add the coconut, chillies, cloves, cinnamon stick and coriander, poppy and cumin seeds, and stir to toast and lightly colour the spices evenly. Watch closely that the coconut does not burn or over-colour. The aroma should be beautiful. Transfer the spices to a spice grinder and grind until a fine powder forms. Set aside.

Cut the lamb into bite-sized pieces, trimming and discarding any fat. Peel and finely chop the ginger.

Melt the coconut oil over a high heat in the sauté pan. Add the chopped ginger and then the lamb and stir together so the lamb browns on all sides and starts cooking. Watch closely so the ginger doesn't burn.

Reduce the heat to medium, add the onion paste and stir it into the oil for 30 seconds. Tip in all the spice powder, add 1 teaspoon of salt and stir so the lamb pieces are well coated. Add the water and bring to the boil, stirring. Cover the pan, turn the heat to low and leave the curry to simmer for 10–12 minutes until the lamb is tender.

Meanwhile, squeeze 1 tablespoon of lime juice. Rinse the coriander sprigs. Set aside 4 sprigs for garnishing and chop enough leaves to make about 1 tablespoon.

When the lamb is tender, stir in the lime juice and chopped coriander. Adjust the seasoning with salt, if necessary, and garnish with coriander sprigs just before serving.

Atul's time-saving tip
In India, this deep, dark curry would most commonly be made with goat or mutton, but I've chosen quick-cooking lamb rump or neck fillet so you can enjoy it within 30 minutes. You can also use quick-cooking beef rump or tenderloin.

MEAT PEPPER FRY

Mattan Pepper Fry

From Kerala, this curry – a very common recipe among the Christians of the region, where it would most likely be made with mutton or goat – has very little gravy. In my catering college, I had lots of classmates from Kerala and they were all experts at cooking curries like this. I was fortunate to learn first-hand from the masters. I owe so much to George; he was an absolutely amazing chef and this was his favourite curry as well. Whenever I'm in Kerala I try to meet up with George because my career owes so much to him.

This is such a different cooking technique than I am used to using in north Indian recipes. There I would fry the ginger first, but here the onions go straight into the pan with the ginger and garlic. Also, cooking in coconut oil gives the dish a totally different taste.

I have actually been very cautious with the black pepper here although it might look like a lot, but if a Keralan chef was making this he or she would add lots and lots of pepper, so feel free to add as much as you like. All you need is some bread to serve with this.

SERVES 4

600g boneless lamb rump or
  neck fillet
2.5cm piece of fresh ginger
4 garlic cloves
2 onions
2 teaspoons black peppercorns,
  or to taste (see introduction,
  above)
fresh coriander leaves
200ml water
2 teaspoons white wine vinegar
1 heaped tablespoon coconut oil
5 fresh or dried curry leaves
2 teaspoons Onion Paste (page 218)
½ teaspoon ground turmeric
sea salt

Assemble all the ingredients and equipment before you begin. You need a spice grinder or pestle and mortar, a large heavy-based saucepan with a lid, a sieve and a large sauté or frying pan.

Cut the lamb into bite-sized pieces, trimming and discarding any fat, then set aside. Peel and finely chop the ginger. Peel and thinly slice the garlic cloves. Peel, halve and thinly slice the onions. Put the peppercorns in a spice grinder, or use a pestle and mortar, to finely grind or crush. Rinse and chop enough coriander leaves to make about 1 tablespoon.

Put the lamb, water, vinegar, ½ teaspoon of the freshly ground pepper and ½ teaspoon of the salt in the saucepan. Cover the pan and bring to the boil, then reduce the heat and leave the meat to simmer at a slow boil for 8 minutes. Strain the meat, reserving the cooking liquid.

Meanwhile, melt the coconut oil over a medium-high heat in the sauté pan. Add the onions, curry leaves, ginger, garlic and a pinch of salt, and stir until the onions are lightly coloured. Add the onion paste and turmeric and stir into the onions for 30 seconds.

Add the meat and stir in half the reserved cooking liquid, which will be absorbed and evaporate quite quickly. Add the remaining liquid a little at a time, stirring, until it mostly evaporates. With the last addition, the gravy should almost be like a thin paste coating the lamb and the lamb should be tender.

Stir in 1 teaspoon of the freshly ground pepper, adjust the seasoning with salt, if necessary, and continue stirring until all the liquid evaporates. Sprinkle with about ½ teaspoon of the ground pepper and the chopped coriander leaves just before serving.

MADRAS LAMB CURRY

Attiraicchi Kari

Old habits die hard. Having grown up eating Madras curries for most of my life, I find it almost impossible to think of going out for a Chenni curry, so I'm sticking with the traditional name here.

As I blended the spice paste in this recipe the aroma was so evocative of my formative years in south India as a young chef. Wherever I went, whether it was to visit with family or friends, I experienced all these smells. I remember them well. Cooking the spice paste with an extra tablespoon of coconut oil simply adds richness to this otherwise simple and straightforward curry from Tamil Nadu. If you reheat leftovers, you will have to stir in a little water because the coconut will have absorbed all the liquid.

SERVES 4

600g boneless lamb rump or
   neck fillet
3 tablespoons coconut oil
2.5cm piece of cinnamon stick
2 tablespoons Onion Paste
   (page 218)
4 tablespoons canned chopped
   tomatoes
250ml water
15 fresh curry leaves
fresh coriander leaves, to garnish
salt

For the spice paste

4cm piece of fresh ginger
6 garlic cloves
4 long thin green chillies
125g desiccated coconut
1 teaspoon ground cinnamon
1 tablespoon ground coriander
2 teaspoons red chilli powder, or
   to taste
1 teaspoon cumin seeds
1 teaspoon fennel seeds
1 teaspoon white poppy seeds
¼ teaspoon black peppercorns
375ml water

Assemble all the ingredients and equipment before you begin. You need a food processor fitted with a chopping blade, a large non-stick sauté or frying pan with a lid, and a wok or another sauté or frying pan.

First make the spice paste. Peel and coarsely chop the ginger. Peel the garlic cloves. Remove the stalks from the green chillies, if necessary. Put the ginger, garlic, chillies, coconut, ground cinnamon, ground coriander, chilli powder, cumin seeds, fennel seeds, poppy seeds, peppercorns and water into the food processor, and blitz, scraping down the sides of the bowl as necessary, until a thick paste forms. Set aside.

Cut the lamb into bite-sized pieces, trimming and discarding any fat.

Melt 2 tablespoons of the coconut oil over a medium-high heat in the sauté pan. Add the cinnamon stick and stir around to flavour the oil, then add the onion paste and stir it into the oil for 30 seconds. Add the lamb, increase the heat to high and stir until browned on all sides. Lower the heat and leave to continue cooking, stirring occasionally, while you cook the spice paste. Watch carefully so the lamb doesn't catch and burn.

Meanwhile, melt the remaining 1 tablespoon of the coconut oil over a medium-high heat in the wok. Add the spice paste and stir for 2 minutes to incorporate the oil and cook all the spices. Stir in the tomatoes and continue simmering for another minute, stirring constantly. Season with salt.

Add the paste mixture to the lamb and stir until all the ingredients are blended. Stir in the 250ml of water. Cover the pan and leave the mixture to gently bubble for 5–8 minutes until the lamb is tender. Adjust the seasoning with salt, if necessary.

Meanwhile, lightly chop the curry leaves and chop enough coriander leaves to make about 2 tablespoons.

Just before serving, stir the curry and coriander leaves into the curry, reserving a few of the coriander leaves to sprinkle over the top.

CAFE-STYLE MEAT CURRY

Thattukada Erachi Kari

Wherever you travel in India, there is always a road-side café serving a basic, simple curry, and this is my version. In north India, we would call this a *dhaba* curry. It's hot and it's spicy. There are no tomatoes, no coconut and no tamarind – just spices, onion paste, lamb meat and the lamb juices. Serve this with rice or bread.

SERVES 4

600g boneless lamb rump or
  neck fillet
4cm piece of fresh ginger
1 long thin green chilli
1 tablespoon coconut oil
2 tablespoons Onion Paste
  (page 218)
12 fresh or dried curry leaves
250ml water
sea salt
fresh coriander sprigs, to garnish

For the spice powder

4cm piece of cinnamon stick
2 green cardamom pods
2 cloves
1 star anise
1 tablespoon ground coriander
1–2 teaspoons red chilli powder, or
  to taste
½ teaspoon fennel seeds
½ teaspoon ground black pepper
½ teaspoon ground turmeric

Assemble all the ingredients and equipment before you begin. You need a spice grinder, a large bowl and a large non-stick sauté or frying pan with a lid.

First make the spice powder. Put the cinnamon stick, cardamom pods, cloves, star anise, ground coriander, chilli powder, fennel seeds, black pepper and turmeric into the spice grinder, and grind until a fine powder forms. Tip the powder into the bowl.

Cut the lamb into bite-sized pieces, discarding any fat. Add the lamb to the spice powder, season with salt and mix together so the lamb pieces are well coated. Set aside.

Peel and finely chop the ginger. Remove the stalk from the green chilli, if necessary, then finely chop the chilli.

Melt the coconut oil over a medium-high heat in the pan. Add the onion paste and stir it into the oil for 30 seconds. Turn the heat to high and stir in the spice-coated lamb with the ginger, green chilli and curry leaves, and stir everything together for 30 seconds to cook the spice powder and brown the lamb. Watch very closely so the spices don't burn.

Stir in the water and bring to the boil. Cover the pan, reduce the heat to low and leave to simmer for 10–12 minutes until the lamb is tender.

Meanwhile, rinse the coriander sprigs for the garnish.

Adjust the seasoning with salt, if necessary, and garnish with coriander sprigs just before serving.

GOAN 'MUTTON' CURRY

Goa Cordeiro Kari

I'm calling this a 'mutton' curry, but it's actually made with lamb. It's just that we're so used to calling lamb 'mutton' in India.

SERVES 4

600g boneless lamb rump or
  neck fillet
2 tablespoons vegetable oil
1 dried red chilli
4 tablespoons Onion Paste
  (page 218)
1 teaspoon Garlic Paste (page 220)
250ml water
fresh coriander leaves
125ml coconut milk
3 tablespoons Tamarind Liquid
  (page 223)
1 teaspoon garam masala
sea salt

For the spice powder

2 large dried red chillies
1 cinnamon stick
2 tablespoons coriander seeds
1 tablespoon cumin seeds
3 tablespoons desiccated coconut

Assemble all the ingredients and equipment before you begin. You need a spice grinder, a non-stick pan for toasting the spices and a large non-stick sauté or frying pan with a lid.

First make the spice powder. Place the dried chillies into the spice grinder. Heat the dry non-stick pan over a high heat. Add the cinnamon and coriander and cumin seeds and stir until the spices are aromatic. Tip them into the spice grinder and grind until a fine powder forms.

Wipe out the pan, then return it to a low heat. Add the coconut and stir until it turns light golden brown. Watch closely so it doesn't burn. Add the coconut to the spice grinder and grind with the powder until finely ground. Set aside.

Cut the lamb into bite-sized pieces, trimming and discarding any fat.

Heat the vegetable oil with the dried chilli over a medium-high heat in the sauté pan. Add the spice powder and stir for 30 seconds. Watch closely so the spices do not burn. Add the onion paste and garlic paste and continue stirring for a further 30 seconds.

Turn the heat to high, add the lamb and continue stirring until it is browned all over. Add the water and season with salt. Reduce the heat, cover the pan and leave the curry to simmer for 8 minutes.

Meanwhile, rinse and chop enough coriander leaves to make about 2 tablespoons.

Stir the coconut milk, tamarind liquid, garam masala and half the chopped coriander into the curry, then leave it to bubble for a further 2 minutes, or until the lamb is tender.

Adjust the seasoning with salt, if necessary, and sprinkle with the remaining chopped coriander to serve.

SPICED LAMB MINCE

Bhuna Keema

It doesn't take long to make this straightforward curry, but it isn't one of those recipes you can just walk away from and leave it to simmer unattended. Once you add the lamb mince to the pan, you need to constantly stir, adding the water gradually and keeping the mixture moving to stop it burning, and to incorporate any crusty bits that develop on the bottom of the pan. This is very important, and is what gives the dish the *bhuna* flavour.

This can also be made with beef mince, and you should serve either version with naan bread.

SERVES 4

4 green cardamom pods
2 black cardamom pods
3 long thin green chillies
2 tablespoons vegetable oil
12 black peppercorns
2 dried bay leaves
3 tablespoons Onion Paste
  (page 218)
500g minced lamb
1 tablespoon ground coriander
1 teaspoon red chilli powder, or
  to taste
1 teaspoon garam masala
1 teaspoon ground turmeric
400ml water
small handful fresh coriander leaves
small handful fresh mint leaves
½ lemon
sea salt

Assemble all the ingredients and equipment before you begin. You need a large non-stick sauté or frying pan with a lid.

Lightly crush the green and black cardamom pods to release the seeds. Cut the green chillies in half lengthways, but do not remove the stalks.

Heat the vegetable oil over a medium-high heat in the pan. Add the green and black cardamom pods and their seeds, the peppercorns and the bay leaves, and stir until the spices crackle. Add the onion paste and stir it into the oil for 30 seconds.

Add the lamb, season with salt and stir to break up the meat and incorporate the onion paste and spices. Add the ground coriander, chilli powder, garam masala and turmeric, and stir for 30 seconds to incorporate and cook the spices. Watch closely and stir constantly so none of the ingredients catch and burn.

Add the green chillies and 100ml of the water, scraping the bottom of the pan and stirring to incorporate any of the caramelised bits on the bottom of the pan. Spread the mixture out in a thin layer with the back of your spatula and leave it to cook until it is slightly caramelised – like a thin crust. Add 250ml of the water and again stir to incorporate the caramelised bits, then leave until the water evaporates.

When the meat is cooked through, stir in the remaining 50ml of water. Cover the pan and leave the mixture to gently bubble for about 5 minutes.

Meanwhile, rinse the coriander and mint leaves. Set aside a few coriander leaves for a garnish, then finely chop all the remaining leaves. Squeeze 1 tablespoon of lemon juice.

Stir the chopped mint and coriander leaves and lemon juice into the lamb mixture and adjust the seasoning with salt, if necessary. Garnish with coriander leaves to serve.

MINCE WITH PEAS

Keema Mutter

The key to getting the Indian-restaurant-favourite out of the pan and on the table within thirty minutes is to get the minced lamb cooking in the water as soon as possible. That way you'll still have time to prep the other ingredients and there will be plenty of time for all the flavours to blend.

I'm using frozen peas here for convenience, but if you have fresh peas, blanch them in a separate pan of salted water while the liquid is evaporating in the frying pan, then quickly refresh them to stop the cooking and set their vibrant green colour. That way they only have to be warmed through at the end, and I always keep a few back for a garnish.

SERVES 4

500g minced lamb or beef
4.5cm piece of fresh ginger
7 black cardamom pods
2 mild green chillies
1 onion
2½ teaspoons garam masala
3 green cardamom pods
2½ tablespoons vegetable oil
6 black peppercorns
4 cloves
1 dried bay leaf
1 teaspoon cumin seeds
2 tomatoes
1 lime
fresh coriander leaves
1 tablespoon ground coriander
1 teaspoon red chilli powder, or
  to taste
1 heaped teaspoon ground turmeric
½ teaspoon dried fenugreek leaf
  powder
3 tablespoons Onion Masala
  (page 222)
200g frozen peas
sea salt

Assemble all the ingredients and equipment before you begin. You need a heavy-based saucepan and a large sauté or frying pan.

Put the lamb mince into the saucepan and season with salt. Add just enough cold water to cover and set the pan over a high heat.

While the water is heating, peel and finely chop the ginger. Lightly crush the black cardamom pods to loosen the seeds. Remove the stalk from both chillies, if necessary, then split one chilli in half lengthways and finely chop the other. Peel, halve and finely chop the onion.

Add half the chopped ginger, 1 black cardamom pod, the slit green chilli and 1 teaspoon of the garam masala to the mince, using a wooden spoon or spatula to break up the meat. Bring to the boil and leave to continue boiling, stirring occasionally, until the meat is about three-quarters cooked through and no lumps remain. It will change colour from pinkish red to pale brown.

Meanwhile, lightly crush the green cardamom pods to loosen the seeds.

Heat the vegetable oil over a medium-high heat in the sauté pan. Add the remaining 6 black cardamom pods with the seeds, all the green cardamom pods with the seeds, the peppercorns, cloves, bay leaf and cumin seeds, and stir until the spices crackle. Add the onion with a pinch of salt and stir occasionally until it is lightly coloured.

While the onion is cooking, coarsely chop the tomatoes. Squeeze the juice from the lime and rinse and chop enough coriander leaves to make about 2 tablespoons.

Add the remaining chopped ginger and the chopped chilli to the pan and stir for 30 seconds. Add the tomatoes, ground coriander, red chilli powder, turmeric, fenugreek powder and the remaining 1½ teaspoons of the garam

continued on page 212

masala to the onion, and stir for 30 seconds to cook the spices. Watch closely so they do not burn.

Very carefully add all the mince and the liquid left in the saucepan to the sauté pan and bring to the boil, stirring. Leave the mixture to bubble for about 1 minute until all the liquid evaporates and the meat is tender. Stir frequently to prevent anything catching on the bottom of the pan.

Stir in the onion masala. Add the frozen peas and the lime juice, and boil for a further 2 minutes, stirring, or until the peas are hot.

Adjust the seasoning with salt, if necessary, then stir in the chopped coriander to serve.

GOAT CURRY

Meat Kolhapuri

The dried red chillies and chilli powder make this a very hot curry. It comes from Kerala, where they grow a lot of chillies so it's not surprising that this is spicy hot.

I grew up eating goat meat and it's really tasty. I love it. Plus, goat meat is fashionable now, with lower cholesterol than either beef or lamb. You'll most likely have to get this from a butcher, but that means you can get it on the bone and cut it into bite-sized pieces. I particularly like cooking meat on the bone, because there is so much more flavour and the meat is so much moister, but the only way to cook with bones quickly is to use a pressure cooker, and even then it will take you closer to 40 minutes for really tender meat.

I know I'm breaking the rule of the 30-minute limit here, but this is such a good curry I really want to include it. Some rules are just made to be broken, don't you think? (Well, as long as it's not the chefs in my restaurant kitchens who are breaking the rules!)

If you can't find the white poppy seeds, don't fuss. They are optional. You could use lamb stock, rather than the water, but there really isn't any need for that.

SERVES 4

750g goat meat on the bone; ask the butcher to saw it into bite-sized pieces for you
2 tablespoons Ginger-Garlic Paste (page 220)
2 teaspoons red chilli powder, or to taste
2 teaspoons garam masala
1½ tablespoons coconut oil
2 large dried red chillies
4 tablespoons Onion Paste (page 218)
fresh coriander leaves, to garnish
sea salt

For the spice powder
4 tablespoons frozen grated coconut
2 teaspoons sesame seeds
2 teaspoons white poppy seeds (optional)

Assemble all the ingredients and equipment before you begin. You need a pressure cooker (page 229), a non-stick pan for toasting the coconut and seeds, a spice grinder and a saucepan if your pressure cooker is a model that can't be placed on the hob.

Place the meat in a bowl. Add the ginger-garlic paste, chilli powder and garam masala, season with salt and mix together so all the meat is coated. Set aside.

Melt the coconut oil in the pressure cooker over a medium-high heat. Add the chillies and stir until they flavour the oil. Add the meat and stir for 30 seconds to sear the meat and cook the spices. Watch closely so the spices do not burn.

Add just enough water to cover the meat by about 2.5cm. Seal the lid and cook over a high heat to bring to high pressure. Reduce the heat to maintain pressure and cook for 20–25 minutes, or according to the manufacturer's instructions.

Meanwhile, make the spice powder. Heat the dry non-stick pan over a low heat. Add the frozen coconut, sesame seeds and poppy seeds, and stir until the coconut turns light golden brown and the sesame and poppy seeds pop. Watch closely so nothing burns, which can happen very quickly.

Transfer the coconut and seeds to the spice grinder and finely grind. Because there is so much oil in the coconut and the seeds, the texture will be a cross between a fine powder and a paste. Set aside.

continued on page 215

Rinse and chop enough coriander leaves to make about 2 tablespoons.

When the meat is cooked, release the pressure according to the manufacturer's instructions and remove the lid. Stir in the spice paste and salt to taste. Place the pressure cooker over a high heat. Bring to the boil, uncovered, and leave to bubble for 3 minutes to evaporate the excess liquid. (If your pressure cooker is a model that can not be used on the hob, then transfer the meat and the sauce to a saucepan before stirring in the spice paste.)

Adjust the seasoning with salt, if necessary, and sprinkle with the chopped coriander just before serving.

BASICS, GLOSSARY, EQUIPMENT AND MEASURES

BOILED RICE

SERVES 4

200g basmati rice
sea salt

Tip the rice into a sieve and rinse under the cold tap until the water runs clear. Transfer to a saucepan with water to cover by 2.5cm and salt to taste. Bring to the boil, then boil for 5–8 minutes until tender. Drain well and keep warm until required, or serve immediately.

ONION PASTE

MAKES ABOUT 600G

2 tablespoons vegetable oil
500g onions, coarsely chopped
100g (about 6 tablespoons) Ginger-Garlic Paste (page 220)
1 teaspoon sea salt

Heat the oil over a medium-high heat in a large sauté or frying pan that is ideally non-stick. Add the onions, the ginger-garlic paste and salt, and stir frequently for 25 minutes, or until the onions are browned. Watch carefully towards the end of cooking so the mixture doesn't catch and burn, which can happen very quickly. If they do burn, you'll have to throw them out and start over – there isn't any way to rescue them.

Transfer the mixture to a food processor while it's still warm and blitz to a fine paste. Leave to cool completely, then store in a covered container in the fridge for up to 4 weeks, or freeze for up to 3 months.

GARLIC PASTE

MAKES ABOUT 200G

2 large garlic heads, 75g each, separated into cloves and peeled
4 tablespoons water
2 tablespoons vegetable oil

Put the garlic cloves, water and vegetable oil in a food processor fitted with a chopping blade and blitz, scraping down the sides of the bowl as necessary, until a paste forms.

This keeps in a covered container in the fridge for up to 4 weeks, or can be frozen for up to 3 months.

GINGER-GARLIC PASTE

MAKES ABOUT 225G

2 large garlic heads, 75g each, separated into cloves and peeled
150g fresh ginger, peeled weight, coarsely chopped
2 tablespoons water

Put the garlic cloves, ginger and water in a food processor fitted with a chopping blade and blitz, scraping down the sides of the bowl as necessary, until a paste forms.

This keeps in a covered container in the fridge for up to 4 weeks, or can be frozen for up to 3 months.

CURRY PASTE

I cringe when I see people buying commercial curry paste in the supermarket. It's not expensive to make your own, and you have control over the ingredients that go into it, which is especially important to me with a young family. I urge you to make even a double batch of this recipe so you always have a supply in the fridge or freezer. The lemon juice or vinegar that is added towards the end of the recipe acts as a preservative so the paste keeps in the fridge for up to a month in a well-covered container.

I don't think it will take you long to appreciate how much flavour this basic recipe has, and how you can use it to transform just about any ingredients you happen to have in the fridge into a satisfying meal in minutes.

MAKES ABOUT 435G

4 tablespoons vegetable oil
2 tablespoons ground coriander
2 teaspoons garam masala
2 teaspoons ground turmeric
1½ teaspoons red chilli powder, or to taste
500g onions, coarsely chopped
100g (about 6 tablespoons) Ginger-Garlic Paste (page 220)
1 teaspoon sea salt
100ml freshly squeezed lemon juice, or white wine vinegar

Heat the oil over a medium-high heat in a large sauté or frying pan. Add the ground coriander, garam masala, turmeric and chilli powder, and stir for 30 seconds to cook the spices. Watch closely so they do not burn.

Add the onions, ginger-garlic paste and salt, and stir frequently for 20 minutes, or until the mixture turns brown. Stirring frequently is important so the onions don't stick to the bottom of the pan. You really have to keep your eyes on the pan, because the onions can burn quickly. If they do there isn't any way to rescue the paste.

Add the lemon juice and continue stirring for 2 minutes, or until the excess liquid evaporates. Transfer the mixture to a food processor while it's still warm and blitz, scraping down the sides of the bowl as necessary, until a fine paste forms.

Leave the paste to cool completely, then store in a covered container in the fridge for up to 4 weeks, or freeze for up to 3 months.

ONION MASALA

Another essential component of many of the recipes in this book, a scaled-down version of my restaurant recipe, for adding flavour in a hurry.

MAKES ABOUT 300G

2 tablespoons vegetable oil
2.5cm piece of cinnamon stick
2 green cardamom pods, lightly crushed
1 teaspoon cumin seeds
1 dried bay leaf
2 onions, finely chopped
1 teaspoon Ginger-Garlic Paste (page 220)
1 teaspoon ground coriander
½ teaspoon ground cumin
½ teaspoon garam masala
½ teaspoon ground turmeric
225ml water
1 tablespoon tomato purée, mixed with 4 tablespoons water
sea salt

Heat the oil over a medium-high heat in a heavy-based saucepan. Add the cinnamon, cardamom pods, cumin seeds and the bay leaf, and stir until the pods crackle. Add the onions and continue stirring until they are lightly coloured. Lower the heat, add the ginger-garlic paste and stir for 2–3 minutes until the raw smell of the paste disappears.

Return the heat to medium-high, add the ground coriander, ground cumin, garam masala and turmeric, and stir for 30 seconds to cook the spices. Watch closely so they do not burn.

Remove and discard the piece of cinnamon and the bay leaf.

Transfer the mixture to a food processor fitted with a chopping blade, add the water and blitz. Add the diluted tomato purée, season with salt and blitz again, scraping down the sides of the bowl as necessary, until blended. Transfer to a saucepan over a medium heat and simmer, uncovered and stirring frequently, for 20–25 minutes until it thickens and turns brown. Watch carefully towards the end of cooking that the mixture doesn't stick to the bottom of the pan. While cooking, it will gloop occasionally and splatter. It can burn or scald, so cook with caution.

Set aside to cool completely, then store in a covered container in the fridge for up to 4 weeks, or freeze for up to 3 months.

TAMARIND LIQUID

Tamarind is used as a tangy souring agent in Indian cookery. The flavour is derived from the pods of the tamarind tree. These are sold as seedless, dried compressed blocks. This pulp needs to be soaked in hot water before use. Ready-made tamarind paste is available, but it is often salty and I think it is better to make your own.

Break up the specified weight of pulp and soak in hot water to cover for about 20 minutes to soften, using your fingers to mix the pods with the water – the tamarind paste will become thicker. Strain through a sieve into a bowl, pressing to extract as much flavour as possible. The proportion of liquid to tamarind pulp varies according to the intensity of flavour required. Allow 400ml water per 200g block. The extracted juice can be stored in the fridge for 2–3 weeks, or frozen and diluted as required.

BENARES CURRY POWDER

This is lighter than the curry powders you buy, which can be heavy with turmeric and chillies. I wanted a blend that lets the taste of the green cardamoms and fennel come through. The Kashmiri chilli powder gives a rich redness without searing heat, and the dried mango powder lends a citrus tang.

MAKES ABOUT 5½ TABLESPOONS

5cm piece of cinnamon stick
10 green cardamom pods
10 cloves
4 dried red chillies
1 tablespoon coriander seeds
1 tablespoon cumin seeds
2 teaspoons fennel seeds
1 teaspoon black peppercorns
1½ teaspoons Kashmiri chilli powder
1½ teaspoons dried mango powder
1½ teaspoons turmeric

Toast the whole spices individually in a dry frying pan over a medium heat until aromatic. Immediately tip them out of the pan into a spice grinder or a mini food processor. Add the ground spices and blitz to a fine powder. Sift through a fine sieve. Store in an airtight container in a dark cupboard for up to 3 weeks.

STORING PASTES

Having a ready supply of these pastes is essential for making many of the curries in this book within 30 minutes. They add great depth of flavour without you having to spend time preparing and cooking individual ingredients. I use these in my restaurants and at home. Fortunately, they have a good storage life in the fridge, and can all be frozen, so you can always be prepared for 30-minute curry cooking.

I recommend you freeze the Ginger-Garlic Paste (page 220) and Onion Paste (page 218) in tablespoon portions, and the Garlic Paste (page 220) in teaspoon portions. Simply put the amount you decide on in moulds of an ice-cube tray and freeze. When the paste is frozen, I then transfer the individual cubes to a freezer bag and label. The cubes can then be added to the recipe straight from the freezer, and you don't have to spend time calculating how much you need.

It's best to buy a very inexpensive ice-cube tray just for freezing pastes – otherwise your gin and tonics will have a very unexpected flavour!

DRY TOASTING SPICES

Spices generally contain a great deal of oil, so if you leave toasted spices to cool slightly before grinding, the powder won't stick to the bottom of the grinder, making washing up easier. Sometimes, when I'm working against the clock, however, this isn't possible.

Whole spices are often toasted before use to intensify their flavour. Once toasted, however, spices lose their flavour quickly, so always toast just before using. Put them in a dry, heavy-based frying pan over a medium heat and toast until they become aromatic and the colour just starts to darken, stirring occasionally or shaking the pan to prevent burning. Tip them out of the pan immediately to stop the cooking.

Dried herbs, such as bay leaves, are often toasted to remove any moisture they might retain before grinding.

Grinding spices is an essential technique, and spices can be ground with or without having been toasted first. Depending on the recipe, it might be dry grinding or wet grinding. When grinding cinnamon sticks and/or cassia bark, an electric spice grinder is the best option, and either spice should be broken into small pieces before grinding. When a fine powder is required, the recipe will specify to sift the ground spices to remove any pieces of bark or shell. For wet grinding, use a blender or a mini food processor. Spices should be ground as specified in the recipe – to a coarse or fine powder, and some spice powders are then sifted for an even finer texture.

GLOSSARY

Writing the recipes for this book has been a voyage of discovery for me. I've been discovering the cooking of India in a way I've never quite appreciated before. I find it fascinating how I use many of the same spices, but they result in such different flavours, depending on the oil they are cooked in, for example. Below is a glossary of the ingredients I use most often in these pages (along with some hints and tips about how to use and prep them).

ASAFOETIDA

This is a dried gum-like resin derived from the ferula (giant fennel plants). It lends an interesting flavour when used in small quantities, but in bulk it releases an overpowering smell. Asafoetida powder contains rice powder to prevent lumping. Use sparingly.

BLACK CUMIN SEEDS

These are more aromatic than the more common brown seeds.

CARDAMOM

These are available as both black and green pods that contain a cluster of small black, fragrant seeds, yet their uses and flavours are very different. The pale green pods have a pleasant, perfume-like aroma and are used in both sweet and savoury dishes, while the hard, black pods have a more pronounced, camphor-like aroma and are only used in savoury dishes. Both varieties should be bruised before toasting or frying in oil to prevent them from exploding, and of course it is good for flavour. I suggest using the flat side of a chef's knife or the back of a large wooden spoon to bruise them. Ground cardamom is made from green cardamom pods; the seeds are lightly toasted and then ground to a powder.

CHILLIES

I dislike fiery hot chillies, so I use green Dutch chillies, which are milder than many varieties. Look for long, plump chillies in supermarkets as well as Asian food shops. In my kitchen, red chillies are always dried, and I prefer Kashmiri red chillies for their flavour and colour. These are big and broad, and are used whole or ground to make Kashmiri chilli powder, which adds a great depth of flavour to dishes, particularly when first added to the cooking oil.

Always check your chillies to see how hot they are before you add them to the curry, because you might want more or less than I suggest. The way I do this is to just cut off a tiny bit of the tip and taste that, then use to your preference, according to how hot you like your food.

COCONUT

I use a lot of frozen grated coconut in the recipes in this book, which is becoming increasingly common in UK supermarkets, otherwise an Asian or Indian shop should stock it. If you can't find frozen grated coconut you could use desiccated coconut, but I'm not a great fan of it. Instead, I suggest you replace the water in the paste with the same amount of coconut milk.

COCONUT MILK

This is prepared from fresh coconut flesh, and should not be confused with the liquid inside a coconut. To prepare coconut milk, soak 500g grated fresh coconut (or frozen, see above) in 300ml lukewarm water for about 30 minutes, then blitz in a blender on high speed for a few minutes. Strain the mixture through a fine-meshed sieve or a muslin-lined strainer. This first extraction should yield about 250ml and is usually called thick coconut milk, simply referred to as coconut milk in my recipes. You can repeat the process with the residue from the first extraction and a further 300ml lukewarm water to make a 'thin' coconut milk. Coconut milk is readily available in cans and long-life packs.

COCONUT OIL

This is extracted from coconut flesh, and because of its high saturated fat content it is solid at room temperature. I often use it for tempering and when cooking seafood. It is sold in supermarkets and provides a totally unique flavour.

CURRY LEAVES

Sold fresh and dried, these are used in many Indian preparations, especially those from the south. I always prefer to use fresh leaves, which you can buy from Asian food shops, but use dried if necessary. Freezing curry leaves preserves their flavour very well. If you buy them fresh you can store them in a plastic airtight container layered with kitchen paper.

FENUGREEK LEAVES

Fenugreek leaves taste very different from fenugreek seeds and the two are not interchangeable. Dried fenugreek leaf powder is available from Asian food shops, or you can grind your own dried leaves in a pestle and mortar, spice or coffee grinder.

FENUGREEK SEEDS

I'm always cautious when I add fenugreek seeds to a dish and you should always use them sparingly, because they can become bitter very fast. If using, cook the fenugreek seeds at the beginning of a recipe until they darken in colour.

GHEE

This clarified butter has long been the main cooking medium of north India, but with a growing awareness of healthy eating, vegetable oil is taking its place. I prefer to cook with sunflower oil, and, when necessary, use a little ghee to enrich a dish. It is sold in supermarkets.

GROUND FENNEL

Usually only available in Indian food shops, this powdered spice is made from toasted and finely ground fennel seeds. I make my own, which will keep in a covered container for up to 3 months. Simply toast the fennel seeds in a dry frying pan, ideally non-stick, over a high heat until aromatic, then cool and finely grind in a spice grinder or coffee grinder that you use only for spices.

JAGGERY AND PALM SUGAR

Jaggery is a coarse, unrefined sugar from the sugar cane plant. It has a distinctive taste and is much less sweet than refined sugar. Palm sugar is made from the sap of various palm trees, such as date and coconut. Both sugars are used to enrich sauces and desserts, and they are largely interchangeable in Indian cookery. If you can't find either, use muscovado sugar.

LENTILS

I use a range of lentils in these recipes, and even though lentils now come packaged and are unlikely to have been sitting in the open, I still recommend rinsing them out of habit. Gram lentils (*channa daal*) – split, matt yellow gram lentils – are the most widely consumed lentils in India, and are available from Asian food shops. They hold their shape when cooked. You can buy roasted *channa daal* from Asian food shops. Yellow split peas make an acceptable substitute, although *channa daal* has a slightly sweeter, nuttier flavour. Toor lentils (*toor daal*) are similar to gram lentils but are much smaller and disintegrate when cooked.

MUSTARD OIL

We don't get pure mustard oil in the UK, so I tend to blend the mustard oil we do find in this country with rapeseed oil.

MUSTARD SEEDS

Mustard seeds must pop when you sauté them in the hot oil – that's the golden rule with mustard seeds.

PANCH PHORON

This unique spice mix is particular to Bengal, in north east India. It comprises equal quantities of five strongly flavoured spices: black onion, fennel, fenugreek and cumin seeds and radhuni, a typical Bengali spice.

PANEER

This fresh, white, vegetarian cheese is common in Asia and often used in Indian dishes.

POMEGRANATE SEED POWDER (ANARDANA)

Sun-dried pomegranate seeds are used to impart a sour flavour to north Indian dishes. You can buy it from Indian food shops, and it doesn't need cooking. If you can't find it, sumac is a good alternative.

TAMARIND

Tamarind is used as a tangy souring agent in Indian cookery. The flavour is derived from the pods of the tamarind tree. These are sold as seedless, dried compressed blocks. Ready-made tamarind paste is available, but it is often salty and I think it is better to make your own (see page 223 for my method).

TOMATOES

In these recipes I often use either canned chopped tomatoes or passata to get the perfect flavour.

EQUIPMENT

Here is a list of essential equipment for the recipes in this collection, all of which is common in any domestic kitchen.

FOOD PROCESSOR
A medium size works well for these recipes, and they mostly require the chopping blade.

NON-STICK PAN
This can be any pan. I have a separate small non-stick frying pan that I use for toasting spices and dry-frying. It's non-stick so there is less likelihood of the spices burning over a high heat, and you need to cook them over a high heat to activate the oils so they become more aromatic.

PRESSURE COOKER
I wouldn't have a kitchen without a pressure cooker; I use it at home and in my restaurant for cooking pulses. In this book I've suggested using it for the goat curry recipe so the meat can be cooked on the bone, for extra flavour. Pressure cookers vary greatly, so it's important to check the instruction manual before using it for any of the recipes in the book.

All the recipes in this book were tested in a 4-litre pressure cooker that can be used on the hob. If your cooker can't be used on the hob, do any of the initial frying in a pan and then transfer the ingredients to the pressure cooker and continue with the recipe. If there is too much liquid after it has been cooked in the pressure cooker, transfer it to a saucepan and boil over a high heat until the desired consistency is reached.

ROASTING TRAY
You don't need anything special, just good quality and heavy-based.

SAUTÉ / FRYING PANS
A good-quality, heavy-based sauté or frying pan is essential, and many recipes require 2 pans, often one that is non-stick and one or two with a lid – tight-fitting lids are essential in some recipes to keep the curry moist.

SPICE GRINDER
You need a good-quality, strong spice grinder for making all the spice powders that give the recipes their individual qualities. Never put liquid ingredients in a spice grinder. Any spice mixture that contains cinnamon stick has to be ground in a food processor instead. A pestle and mortar is a suitable alternative to a spice grinder, but is often more time consuming.

WOK
Some of my recipes use a wok with a cover, but if you don't have one a large sauté or frying pan with a lid is always given as the alternative.

CONVERSION TABLES

WEIGHTS

Metric	Imperial
15g	½oz
20g	¾oz
30g	1oz
55g	2oz
85g	3oz
110g	4oz / ¼lb
140g	5oz
170g	6oz
200g	7oz
225g	8oz / ½lb
255g	9oz
285g	10oz
310g	11oz
340g	12oz / ¾lb
370g	13oz
400g	14oz
425g	15oz
450g	16oz / 1lb
1kg	2lb 4oz
1.5kg	3lb 5oz

LIQUIDS

Metric	Imperial
5ml	1 teaspoon
15ml	1 tablespoon or ½fl oz
30ml	2 tablespoons or 1fl oz
150ml	¼ pint or 5fl oz
290ml	½ pint or 10fl oz
425ml	¾ pint or 16fl oz
570ml	1 pint or 20fl oz
1 litre	1¾ pints
1.2 litres	2 pints

LENGTH

Metric	Imperial
5mm	¼in
1cm	½in
2cm	¾in
2.5cm	1in
5cm	2in
10cm	4in
15cm	6in
20cm	8in
30cm	12in

OVEN TEMPERATURES

°C	°C Fan	Gas Mark	°F
110°C	90°C Fan	Gas Mark ¼	225°F
120°C	100°C Fan	Gas Mark ½	250°F
140°C	120°C Fan	Gas Mark 1	275°F
150°C	130°C Fan	Gas Mark 2	300°F
160°C	140°C Fan	Gas Mark 3	325°F
180°C	160°C Fan	Gas Mark 4	350°F
190°C	170°C Fan	Gas Mark 5	375°F
200°C	180°C Fan	Gas Mark 6	400°F
220°C	200°C Fan	Gas Mark 7	425°F
230°C	210°C Fan	Gas Mark 8	450°F
240°C	220°C Fan	Gas Mark 9	475°F

USEFUL CONVERSIONS

1 tablespoon = 3 teaspoons
1 level tablespoon = approx. 15g or ½oz
1 heaped tablespoon = approx. 30g or 1oz
1 egg = 55ml / 55g / 2fl oz

INDEX

INDEX

ABOUT THE AUTHOR

Atul Kochhar is one of the world's leading chefs and is the man behind the Michelin-starred restaurant, Benares, in the heart of London's Mayfair. He has restaurants around the world, and has appeared on shows such as BBC's *Saturday Kitchen* and *Great British Menu*. This is his fifth book.

Publisher Jon Croft
Commissioning Editor Meg Avent
Project Editor Emily North
Art Direction Kim Musgrove
Designers Kim Musgrove, Allison Curtis and Marie O'Mara
Cover Designer Nathan Shellard
Editor Beverly leBlanc
Proofreader Rachel Malig
Photographer Mike Cooper
Home Economist Susanna Tee
Indexer Zoe Ross

Absolute Press
An imprint of Bloomsbury Publishing Plc

50 Bedford Square   1385 Broadway
London   New York
WC1B 3DP   NY 10018
UK   USA

www.bloomsbury.com

ABSOLUTE PRESS and the A. logo are trademarks of Bloomsbury Publishing Plc

First published 2017

British Library Cataloguing-in-Publication Data
A catalogue record for this book is available from the British Library.

Library of Congress Cataloguing-in-Publication data has been applied for.

ISBN: HB: 9781472937773
ePDF: 9781472937766
ePub: 9781472937759

2 4 6 8 10 9 7 5 3 1

Printed and bound in China by C&C Offset

Bloomsbury Publishing Plc makes every effort to ensure that the papers used in the manufacture
of our books are natural, recyclable products made from wood grown in well-managed forests.
Our manufacturing processes conform to the environmental regulations of the country of origin.

To find out more about our authors and books visit www.bloomsbury.com. Here you will find
extracts, author interviews, details of forthcoming events and the option to sign up for
our newsletters.

Cook's notes: egg sizes are specified where they are critical, otherwise they are assumed
to be medium.